GOOD IN A CRISIS

Good in a Crisis

A Memoir

Margaret Overton

BLOOMSBURY

LONDON · BERLIN · NEW YORK · SYDNEY

First published in Great Britain 2012

Bloomsbury Publishing Plc
50 Bedford Square
London
WC1B 3DP

www.bloomsbury.com

Bloomsbury Publishing, London, Berlin, New York and Sydney

A CIP catalogue record for this book is
available from the British Library

ISBN 978 1 4088 2435 1

10 9 8 7 6 5 4 3 2 1

Typeset by Westchester Book Group
Printed in Great Britain by Clays Ltd, St Ives plc

*For
Elizabeth
and
Jocelyn*

Never waste the opportunities offered by a good crisis.

—NICCOLÒ MACHIAVELLI

Author's Note

My story begins with a divorce. The divorce precipitated a series of midlife events that happened to someone who'd always presumed she was safe. How I muddled through is part of this tale, certainly not anything I'd prescribe to friends or family or even total strangers, merely a description of personal evolution on a very small scale.

The names of the living have been changed. Details, events, and identifying characteristics have been altered out of kindness or to protect the privacy of those involved. Some characters represent composites of two or more individuals. Dialogue has been reconstructed to the best of my recollection.

—Margaret Overton

Introduction

THE OPERATING ROOM secretary stopped me as I strode past the control desk wearing Gumby-green scrubs and a long blue paper gown. "Hey, Dr. Overton, did you get that page from the CCU?"

"Yeah, thanks, Mario. I went up there for a code." I walked into the storeroom where I restocked the drugs and equipment I'd used at the code blue, then heaved the emergency airway bag up onto its shelf.

It was Memorial Day, and I was on call for the anesthesia department. I had just pronounced someone dead in the Coronary Care Unit. The dead someone was forty-nine, which also happened to be my age.

Call started out well. I'd had a large coffee with cream and a double-chunk chocolate muffin, an indulgence I allowed myself only when I knew I had to work twenty-four hours straight. Or after I'd worked twenty-four hours straight. But then I got that page. It goes without saying that when a person gets struck down in the prime of life, and by prime I mean the age I happen to be at the time, massive empathy ensues. I felt terrible.

I glanced at the clock. It wasn't even noon yet, and I still had twenty hours of call left.

In a big busy hospital such as ours, people die, all the time, every day. It's depressing. But still, someone my age had just died, on a holiday weekend, and I considered it to be a bad omen for the rest of my call.

I am the type of person who searches constantly for signs, symbols, patterns, coincidences, and metaphors. Outside, indoors, during totally random events, I'm usually alert and wondering what it all means. Unfortunately, death isn't a sign or a symbol; it takes you straight beyond metaphor. Death leaves you with nothing but reality.

When I walked through the door of CCU number seven and saw the patient—despite the chaos with all the equipment and noise and the hoopla and mayhem of the nurses and residents and respiratory therapists and medical students and God only knows who else stuffed into that room trying to resuscitate the poor man, drawing up drugs, shocking him, pumping on his chest—the first thing I noticed was that he looked exactly like my dead best friend and former partner in anesthesia, Paul.

I stopped briefly, just inside the door, with the massive airway bag slung over my shoulder, and felt spooked by the resemblance. Paul had been my go-to guy, the person I relied upon to make sense of this morass of a career. He was my thrice-divorced tennis buddy and God-brother. *Paul, snark-master.* Most important, he'd suffered a huge myocardial infarction at the age of forty-nine on Memorial Day eleven years earlier, though he survived it initially. So I felt this weird vibe going on. Memorial Day, heart attacks, forty-nine—the coincidences were swirling.

Tall and bald with a stubby nose and a gap between his front teeth, the patient that morning was nice-looking if you ignored the blue tint to the skin. Death detracts from one's looks, as it should, probably, from an evolutionary perspective. I saw the resemblance to Paul more from the side than from the top down.

I glanced at my scrub shirt. A sticker with the patient's name, date of birth, bar code, and medical record number had attached itself to me. Or perhaps I placed it there, second nature.

Jeremiah Sender. I pulled the sticker off and folded it in half. I wondered if he called himself Jere. Jeremiah and Paul might have been brothers; the resemblance was so striking.

I thought back to that day eleven years before. Paul had phoned in the middle of his heart attack to say he'd driven himself to the closest ER, which was All Saints Hospital; he asked what I knew about the heart surgeons there. I remember where I was sitting when I got the call—on an ivory and white *matelassé* lounge chair in the bedroom, overlooking our backyard. This was back in my Pollyanna days, in those Days Before Divorce. DBD. Before divorce changed everything. Before it changed the way I think. I heard a lot of bad news sitting on that lounge chair—my dad's cancer, Mom telling me an "elephant" was sitting on her chest, a friend checking into rehab. I think I got a few ninth-step phone calls on that lounge chair; I gladly let Stig take it during the divorce. Anyway, a couple of days later, I drove Paul's daughter Linea to see him in the hospital.

"What's a balloon pump, Margaret?" she asked me. Paul had had a big heart attack, requiring what is properly known as an intra-aortic balloon pump, a mechanical device that is used in very sick cardiac patients.

"It's hard to explain, but basically it's a machine that reduces the workload of the heart while supporting the circulation. Kind of like what a friend does in a crisis."

Linea was tall and fair, with a dry sense of humor, just like her dad, and polite, unlike her dad. She babysat for my kids when they were young, and I often came home from a dinner with Stig to find Paul in my family room, feet up on the coffee table, keeping his daughter company while she earned spending money.

"I'm scared," Linea said, her head turned to gaze out the side window. "I don't want him to die."

"I know. But . . . he's getting good care, honey. And he's tough," I said. He was so tough that the thought had never occurred to me he might not survive.

Besides, he was too irreverent to die. Paul used to take the newspaper to church. He kept it handy in case the homily bored him. He had no shame. I loved that about him. Somebody like that absolutely could not die.

Still, it shocked me to see him lying in Intensive Care, attached to the balloon pump. Doctors make terrible patients. Paul irritated the nurses, bossed them around. He told them what drugs to give and how quickly to push them through the IV. When I visited, they took me aside to complain about him, as if that would help. I sympathized but said they should see him at work, at his best, where he was really a pain in the ass. Irritable, bossy, but wickedly funny. I used to leave Caramel Creams on his anesthesia machine when he wasn't looking, a misbegotten attempt to sweeten his disposition. He was stoic, though, lying in ICU. Really tough. I did not see any fear in him. And later, after the coronary bypass surgery, when he went home from the hospital, his behavior was restrained—odd for him, I thought, in a way I understand better now. He seemed . . . haunted, as though he'd seen something and wasn't sure he liked the looks of it. His expression held distance, distraction. I suspect it was the bullet dodged that put that look on his face. And the understanding that everything you think you know, everything you count on, can change in a heartbeat.

I guess that's the essence of middle age. You learn that lesson. Some of us learn it over and over and over.

Chapter One

On Memorial Day 2002 I woke up and decided to leave my husband. I refer to him as my husband, but my best friends Hayley and Kate often referred to him as the Sperm Donor. I always thought that seemed harsh until I decided that seemed right.

There was only one argument, really, that I remember. In mid-November 2001, on a Sunday morning, Stig called to ask what I was doing that day. He'd been up early, making rounds at the hospital.

"Thanksgiving is Thursday," I said. "There's a lot to do. I've got to bring the decorations and turkey dishes up from the storage locker, and I was going to take the boxes that are piled up in the dining room downstairs, get them out of the way. We've got about sixteen coming. I thought this might be a good time to get some of the dead plants off the terrace also."

He didn't say anything.

"You know, the service elevator is broken," I said. The passenger elevator didn't go all the way to the basement. That meant that the boxes had to be carried down a flight of stairs. Some of them I couldn't lift. I knew I couldn't lift the dead plants off the terrace.

"How dare you?"

"Excuse me?"

"Don't nag me. How dare you ask me to help you? I bring home the bacon! Don't ever forget that! I bring home the fucking bacon! And I don't ever want to be asked to help do anything around the house, not ever again! Do you understand that?"

I hung up the phone. My hands shook.

The rage in his voice was out of proportion to a few boxes to be carried to the basement. And who said stuff like "I bring home the bacon"? It was irrelevant. I'd worked or been in school our entire marriage. As had he.

But it was a pivotal event. He stopped talking to me. And I stopped sleeping.

I'd stopped bringing home any bacon three years earlier, when our housekeeper/babysitter left suddenly, my dad died, and I broke my arm, all of which occurred within a six-week period. Those events traumatized our daughters, Bea and Ruthann, as well as me, and I felt I needed to give the girls more time and attention than my job allowed. So I took a leave of absence and signed up for classes in a part-time graduate program while they were at school.

The next year we moved from our house in the suburbs to a condo in the city. Stig hated the "fishbowl" of suburban life; he found it confining.

We bought an old, glorious penthouse in Chicago, filled with light and tall ceilings. The kids took to the new life immediately, adapting with a deftness I envied. But I had trouble adjusting to city living; I didn't belong, I didn't know anyone. I didn't get it— the grocery shopping, the dry cleaning; I couldn't find stuff. The streets were all one way, parking didn't exist, and when I tried to do my errands on foot, I wore myself out. Our dog Olga hated it too. She missed her yard. Shortly after the move downtown I tore the ligaments in my knee and had to have an ACL reconstruction. I was miles instead of minutes from my newly widowed mother, miles away from my friends, lost without a garden. I no longer had the job that had always defined me; my daughters were busy with high school. And from the time we moved away from the "fishbowl" of suburban living that confined Stig and comforted me, it seemed he came home even less frequently.

One evening in early 2002, he called to say he would pick up Ruthann and me for dinner. She was a sophomore in high school at the time. Bea was now a freshman at college. I had a few months remaining to finish my graduate work.

"That's weird," Ruthie said. "Do you think he thinks it's one of our birthdays? Maybe he's confused." We rarely ate together.

When we got in the car, I asked him about his day. He turned up the radio and didn't answer.

The next afternoon Ruthann said, "Mom, let's go for a walk."

We live in a neighborhood north of downtown Chicago called Lakeview. It is a nice mix of young and old, straight and gay, cross-dressing and not. We walked with Olga past some buildings with For Rent notices. Ruthie went over to a sign posted on a two-flat and read out loud.

"Two bedrooms, two baths, fourteen hundred dollars a month. What's A slash C mean?"

"Air conditioning."

"We can do it, Mom. We can afford fourteen hundred a month, can't we?"

I started to cry.

Ruthie turned around and looked at me. "I don't ever want to see what he did to you last night happen again. I don't ever want to see you silenced again. When you started to speak, and he turned up the radio, I thought, That's it. We're moving out."

I nodded. She took my arm, and we walked on.

But it took me another few months. I couldn't figure out the logistics. I didn't have money of my own—he'd made sure of that. Then miraculously my old anesthesia group called and offered me a job. Just like that. It would be part time, to start, working only at the surgical center. I would not be a partner, as I'd been in the past. Three days a week, then possibly more. I would start in six months, but I said yes. Yes! It did not take long before I figured out the rest. My plan had been to wait until Ruthie left for college, but one day I knew that was wrong. We could no longer wait. I was no role model to her or to Bea, waiting.

It's always been like that for me. I equivocate, hesitate, sometimes for years, then *bam!* Clarity strikes, out of the blue. Well, maybe not clarity, exactly. Maybe resolve struck me. Whatever it was, it struck hard on Memorial Day.

Stig had been out of town, Europe I think, and returned that afternoon. We had a barbecue to attend at Hayley and Daniel's house in Winnetka, Illinois. Stig wanted me to pick him up from the airport, then drive him to Winnetka.

"Why don't you take a cab?" I asked. We'd barely spoken in two months. I didn't think he wanted quality time with me in the car. It surprised me he would even go to the party. These were my friends.

"You aren't willing to pick me up from the airport?"

It was a test, I was failing, and I no longer cared.

"I'm working," I said. "I'm in the middle of something, and I'd like to keep going." The man was a surgeon. He could afford a taxi.

When I arrived at the party, I stood between Hayley and Kate.

The three of us have worked together for two decades. I remember hearing the words come out of my mouth: "I'm going to leave him." Once I said them out loud, that was it. My words had weight, and intent. I realized, as I said them, that I'd given myself permission. Finally I felt free.

Kate turned to her husband Neal and whispered in his ear.

"I'm sorry, Margaret," Neal said, then he hugged me.

"Don't be," I answered. "It's time."

Why hadn't I left him when I'd found an article of women's clothing in the backseat of my car ten years earlier? I guess I wasn't ready. When I confronted him with the garment, he admitted everything. The woman was his scrub nurse. Let's give the man snaps for originality.

Stig told me that the reason he cheated that time was that I'd emasculated him by buying myself a rabbit swing coat on sale for $600 from Henri Bendel, when they first opened on Michigan Avenue.

I found this explanation confusing. I'd earned the money. Perhaps I had unknowingly married an herbivore? Was he a meat-eating, leather-wearing closet PETA member all those years, and I hadn't known? Why wasn't he emasculated when I paid the mortgage? Did his girlfriend wear bunny ears?

But he groveled, so I stuck it out, wore the coat, sold the car, and thought he'd cleaned up his act.

On the way home from the party, I asked Stig if he was having an affair. It would have explained a lot.

"No," he shouted. "Are you?"

I looked out the window and did not bother to answer. It

occurred to me that one might identify the end of a relationship by the sheer volume of what's left unsaid.

I waited a few days after clarity struck, then wrote him a letter stating I would not be joining him on our upcoming twentieth-anniversary hiking trip to the Alps. I would be moving out instead. Both girls had summer programs lined up; Bea was attending summer school, Ruthann would be going to camp.

I put the letter on his desk. Talking to him directly never worked out as planned. Plus I'd stopped sleeping in our bedroom and seldom saw him if and when he came home. Stig now wanted to sell the condo. Since my job would start in October, I knew it was my chance to make the break.

After I gave him the letter suggesting a separation, he did not respond.

One morning I walked into our bedroom. He sat at the pine desk, working on his laptop. He quickly closed it when he saw me.

Our bedroom was lovely—we could afford good taste, as we had both made decent money for a number of years. A pleated-silk bed skirt brushed the floor, and a linen throw covered the bed. We had plantation shutters on the windows. Above the bed hung a pine carving, an antique piece with two wooden hearts intertwined. A huge poster of a Renoir painting depicting two young girls hung beside the desk—a redhead and a blonde, just like our daughters. Piles of books covered every available surface. An armoire hid the television, and the *matelassé* lounge chair was beside the bed. I stood near the lounge, then sat.

"What do you think about the separation?" It had been two weeks since I'd given him the letter.

I studied him. He was a stocky man, compact and firm. He wore baggy jeans, and his shirt collar was too loose. He'd lost weight. As an anesthesiologist, I notice things others might not. Like jaw length, neck motion, human density. It's density that interests me, because it's something we pay attention to but don't discuss. Dense people tend to be heavy, or they can be muscular. Men carry their fat on the inside, in the belly region, and with age they tighten up, develop jowls, and lose flexibility. Loose people can be fat or thin, but their bodies move around more easily. Stig was dense, more so when he was heavy. But now he wasn't just dense, he was tight and hiding something. It's easier to take care of loose people in the operating room, regardless of their weight. My guess is that it's better to be loose in life.

Stig didn't say anything for a long moment. He just stared at me, and I thought that he looked like someone I'd never seen before. His hair looked the same, but he'd grown a goatee, along with half the men in America. And his expression—I don't know how to put it except that it seemed scrunched, pinched, so taut that no blood could flow to the surface. His face held rage. And I had no idea where it came from. I suspected it was existential rage. I suspected he was as lost to himself as he was to me.

"That's fine," he said, sealing the fate of our marriage in a single syllable. He nodded. "Fine." One word.

Twenty years, two children, and that was it. No discussion, just . . . fine.

I started to say something, but then thought better of it. I nodded and left the room.

A few days later I moved to our weekend house in Michigan. Stig went on the hiking trip without me.

Clarity, as I've come to understand, is not contagious.

"Are you filing for divorce?" I asked him. Over the phone. We never saw each other.

"I figured you were going to, so I beat you to it," he answered. Stig liked to compete whenever possible. So I borrowed money from my mother for a lawyer.

When I came back to the city to meet with a Realtor, the building engineer mentioned that my husband's girlfriend looked, from behind, just like one of my daughters. That was how I found out he had a girlfriend. He'd been bringing her over while I was living in Michigan. I spent my summer there while he hiked in the Alps, drove around Lake Michigan with his girlfriend, and played golf.

Chapter Two

I REMEMBER PAUL lying in the ICU bed after his heart surgery, eyes shut, a grin on his face.

"You remind me of my ex-wife," he said.

"Which one?" I asked sweetly.

"All of them," he answered. "All three of them."

I knew he meant to insult me—we had that kind of relationship. No one wants to remind anyone of an ex-anything. But in retrospect I tried to look at the bigger picture, especially in light of my own subsequent divorce.

My divorce was brutal, traumatizing, and awful. And I'm just summarizing to make a point. My friend Paul had divorced three times by the age of forty-nine. I can't imagine what he went through. Looking back on this now, from a medical perspective and through the lens of my own experience, I think, as a physician, maybe divorce killed him. Maybe it broke his heart permanently.

One of my many *aha*s over the past few years has been this: medicine organizes my thinking. There's an old teaching adage among general surgeons with regard to acute appendicitis that states, if

you don't take out some normal appendices, you're probably missing a few diseased ones along the way. The underlying rationale is
that not every case of acute appendicitis presents with a classical
picture, and without a high index of suspicion around patients
with nonclassical symptoms, some patients with acute disease may
be missed. There's actually scientific evidence to back up this line
of thinking.

Of course, I'm not a general surgeon; I'm an anesthesiologist.
By the time I see the patient, the decision to remove the appendix
has already been made. But I like this adage from a metaphorical
perspective.

When I was married, if I'd had even a moderately high index of
suspicion, I might have gotten rid of my husband instead of waiting as long as I did, which is to say, I waited so long as to never
have a single moment of regret when I finally left him. Not one.
Not even a nanosecond. Had I left him ten years earlier, when the
kids were young, after only one or so affair, I might have wavered
a bit. But I waited so long . . . well, let's just say that uncertainty
was never my issue. The signs were all there. He fit not just the
classical picture of a cheating husband but the nonclassical one,
the neoclassical one, you name it. The only thing he didn't do was
admit it. Until he was under oath.

There's another old adage I remember from medical school that
seems appropriate with regard to my marriage: If it looks like a
horse, whinnies like a horse, smells like horse pucky, and stomps
its big old freakin' hoof like a horse, chances are it isn't a zebra. My
marriage was nothing if not a dead horse.

Despite fifty years of living, there are certain things I don't get and
probably never will. I could never remember my father's birthday;

I am forever looking up the coagulation cascade, which describes how blood clots; *lay* and *lie* continually bewilder me; and I cannot remember which is which: number one or number two. These are manageable, however. Reference materials or my children provide easy answers. But nothing on Wikipedia, no advanced Google search, no day spent in the Newberry Library, has ever taught me *how men think*.

Sundar was an ENT surgeon I'd worked with for years. His good looks and long eyelashes did nothing to compensate for his constant whining and needling of the nursing staff; procedures with Sundar seemed to last forever. And so I spent what felt like a year with him one day, doing several cases in a row. I sat quietly and unobtrusively completing paperwork as Sundar tortured the scrub nurse, May, and the circulating nurse, Yolanda, from a rolling chair at the patient's head.

"This isn't my suture, May. Where's my regular suture?"

"Doctor, this is four-oh suture, which is what you always use. It's what's listed on your preference card; you used it last week. You use it every time you come to this surgical center, and you say the same thing every time. I'm not certain why you think it looks different again today, but it is not."

"It seems different. *I know* it's different."

"I assure you it is the same suture you always use. The same suture you always complain about."

"Where's the foot pedal for the coblator? *YOLANDA!* I want the foot pedal."

"The switch is on the floor by your left foot, doctor, where it always is. We have not moved it," Yolanda replied.

"Then why can't I find it?"

"Can you find your left foot, doctor?"

"Why do you make *doctor* sound like a dirty word, Yolanda?"

"I'm certain I have no idea what you mean. Doctor."

"Where's the fucking coblator pedal?"

"Oh for God's sake, Sundar," I said, "lift your left foot." I reached down and slid the foot pedal one inch so that it was underneath his shoe. "There. Ya got it?"

"Thanks, Margaret. Thank God someone is helping me."

Days with Sundar were always like this. I rolled my eyes. May rolled her eyes. Yolanda rolled her eyes. During sinus cases performed with the lights out, it became more difficult and less effective to roll our eyes. But he was the master of ceremonies and his wishes took precedence.

In the operating room, idle chitchat is the norm. At some point during the course of the day, Sundar realized I'd gotten a divorce, either through my conversation with May or through the OR rumor mill.

"So where are you living these days, Margaret?" he casually asked.

I explained I'd moved from one condo into another. I told him about the neighborhood, which is well known for its restaurants as well as its proximity to Lincoln Park and the lakefront.

"You know, I sometimes come down to your neighborhood to run along the lakefront, then stop for breakfast at Sheila's. Have you ever eaten there?" Sundar asked.

This is where I made my first of many errors: I answered his question. And I answered truthfully. I do this often. It routinely works to my disadvantage.

"I love Sheila's," I answered, because it is true. "It's close by, and they make the best blueberry pancakes. My neighbor and I have breakfast there a lot."

"Yeah, the omelets are great too. But I especially like the pancakes after a run. How about if I call you some Sunday morning, after I'm done running, and if you're not doing anything, we can meet there and grab breakfast? I'll just give you a call. If you're free, fine. If not, no big deal."

"Sure," I said, and thought to myself, *Why not? This isn't a problem because it will never happen. It is the sort of thing people say, but do not actually do.* In fact, I counted on it.

Four days later, on Sunday, I found myself sitting across from Sundar at Sheila's. Several things struck me. The first was that he had gone home to shower and shave and ditch the stinky running clothes. Considering that he lives thirty miles due west, he either got up at four A.M. or is a very fast runner. I'd been snookered.

The second thing that struck me was Sundar's behavior. He oozed charm. He had a sense of humor. He smiled a lot, and in comparison to the way he acted in the OR, he seemed absolutely lovely. These two things combined led me to believe that, contrary to my wishes in this matter, *I was on a date.*

Now, this was not the first time I'd been on a date that came as a surprise to me. It happened with some frequency due to a certain cluelessness that we'll get into later or that may be obvious by now. So I tried to utilize the experience for educational purposes. What could I learn from this breakfast with Sundar that I had not previously known?

As Sundar chattered away about this and that—about movies he'd seen, plays he'd enjoyed, trips he'd taken, and new restaurants he'd tried, all the while smiling, laughing, and behaving like a complete stranger in a familiar body—it occurred to me that an alien with snakelike allure had taken his form. The man I worked with had been temporarily displaced by this freakishly charismatic individual who sat across from me trying to win my favor. I barely heard him. I kept remembering the way he'd behaved for twenty years in the operating room, and how that contrasted with the person he was right this very minute, because he wanted something.

We left the restaurant, and Sundar immediately texted me. I didn't respond. He called again a week later, but I didn't pick up.

In retrospect, it is not *how men think* that escapes me. I have always understood *how men think*. I just couldn't believe that I knew what I knew.

Yoshie's divorce rivaled mine in duration, expense, and antipathy. We are neighbors, but I am a few years older, a few years past her in the process. I see elements of myself in her, and therefore she drives me completely crazy.

I avoid her at the garbage cans and around the gas grills in summer, not because I dislike her—I don't exactly—but because I am a sympathetic listener. Whenever Yoshie sees me, she natters on about her divorce. I do my best to retain none of the details. But her nattering reinforces what I already know: by its very nature divorce is a public tearing asunder. The combatants lose their filters and boundaries, as well as any sense of time. So Yoshie talks about her divorce until my ears bleed. Ergo, my avoidance behavior.

Not only does Yoshie talk about her divorce ad nauseam, she simultaneously turns into a real alien, à la *Men in Black*. Her ears rotate posteriorly and emit smoke, her voice drops six octaves, and she becomes possessed by a dark force that only people who have been through the divorce process recognize.

I call it helpless, hopeless rage, enabled if not encouraged by the legal system.

Rage, over years, under ordinary circumstances, should make a person ugly, haggard. But as is often the case with divorcing women and men, they actually get better looking. Unless they were the instigator, or the one cheating. That's another story.

Yoshie has long black hair and a curvy figure. She is stunning in a soft, feminine way. She puts on spandex running clothes to go for a five-mile run along the lakefront, and heads swivel the entire time. Even I—a heterosexual female physician—am not certain how a body shaped so much like a Barbie doll can be simultaneously athletic. I'd always thought, and this may be a by-product of reading feminist literature throughout adolescence, that if Barbie were actually a human being, she would topple over. After meeting Yoshie—and seeing her in spandex—I realized this was incorrect.

Recently I ran into Yoshie in front of our building.

"Margaret!"

"Hey Yoshie," I said. "I haven't seen you in ages." I did not mention the garbage can avoidance technique. "What's up?"

"I've been traveling, and I'm applying for a job—this is really exciting! It's with the Coppola organization."

"Francis Ford Coppola?" I asked.

"That's the one! He has a hotel chain, and I'm being interviewed to work with the development team."

"Wow," I responded. I wished I had an interesting job. I wished I could wear nice clothes, eat in restaurants, travel more, see daylight, exercise regularly, not always have to deal with so many bodily juices, and not do so much freaking paperwork. Anything creative or outside of medicine seems exotic and wonderful to me. Yoshie always meets such interesting people.

"So I decided that before I met him, I should probably rent some of his movies—kind of understand the gestalt . . ."

I nodded. Cool. I have no skills that could land me a job with F. F. Coppola unless he needed a hernia repair or a Heimlich maneuver.

"I decided to start with *Apocalypse Now*. Have you ever seen it?"

I shook my head. "Actually, I haven't," I said. "I don't like violence." I see the consequences of violence at the hospital every day. I work at a level-one trauma center in the Chicago area, and we get everything. Knife wounds, gunshot wounds, industrial trauma, car accidents, domestic violence, kids without helmets who've flown off motorcycles, you name it, not to mention the havoc that nature wreaks on the just plain unlucky. So I don't watch *ER*, or *Scrubs*, or other doctor shows because that shit is my life. Enough already.

"Well, I never saw it either. Same thing—I don't like violence. But," Yoshie's eyes widened as she grabbed my arm, "the violence is metaphorical! I still have the movie, I rented it for five days, so I'll give it to you. Margaret, you are going to love this movie! It's all about divorce!"

I smiled, doubtful. *Apocalypse Now* is really about divorce? I thought it was about the insanity of war . . . and drugs . . . and isolation. Senseless violence. Hmmm. I had nothing to do that night, a Saturday on a summer holiday weekend. I might as well watch a good movie.

Yoshie loaned me the Redux version. I put on sweatpants and a T-shirt, ordered a thin-crust organic pizza to be delivered, and settled into the sofa in my family room with a glass of Chardonnay and my sweet mutt Olga curled up next to my feet. Three and a half hours later, the credits rolled, and I smiled.

That Yoshie, I thought. She's onto something. She's only partially correct, though I still hope she gets the job.

Apocalypse Now is a metaphor for divorce, all right. But it also feels like a metaphor for my entire life these past six years. Not just the divorce but everything that followed. The divorce was merely the beginning, when I started heading up the river, into the craziness, looking for Colonel Walter E. Kurtz.

The horror! The horror!

If I made the movie, I might have named it *Apocalypse Right This Very Damned Minute and for as Long as You Can Possibly Imagine*, since it's about my life. I guess that's why I'm in medicine and not in the movie business.

But I have learned four things about divorce during my sojourn on the river. I call them the four admonishments. I've learned them the hard way, having made every mistake I speak of. So here goes . . .

When we tell our side of the story on the phone, in person, in whispers, even via attorneys, in the yard, at work, in the school parking lot, or at the neighborhood Starbucks, and talk about the soon-to-be-ex in tones that are unmistakably angry, even vicious, our children, whatever age they may be, including full-grown adult children, are completely unprotected.

Our job, as parents, is to protect our children. And during a divorce, we don't do that. We become our first priority. That's not easy to change when we're hurting. But they overhear. Everything.

This overhearing may be firsthand, or secondhand, through a closed door or across several states. But it affects kids for the rest of their lives. It affects their future relationships with you, with your ex, with their significant others, and even with their own children. So watch what you say.

People going through a divorce inflict collateral damage. Think bombs, hand grenades, napalm in the morning. This is because we are crazy. I cannot stress this enough. We hurt others. We do crazy things. We can rationalize anything. We buy stupid cars. We date stupid people. We are cruel. We think having sex or quickly replacing the ex with another will solve all our problems. We will hurt you, even if or especially if you are one of us, with or without therapy. When I was going through this, I hurt people. And they hurt me. Now I want to offer my counsel: leave everyone with a heart alone. And as soon as you think you are ready, you've moved on, it's behind you—that is when you are at your most dangerous! All people going through a divorce should have neon arrows mounted over their heads, which announce their arrival. Buyer beware.

The process of divorce requires that we develop a narrative, an attempt to sum up the "truth" of the marriage and its dissolution, as if things might be put straight in some cosmic manner with enough words, delivered just so, to enough people, with just the right emphasis. Believe me, constant repetition of the narrative will bore the crap out of your friends until their eyes cross and they fall asleep standing up.

What's the truth? The truth is what happened between you and him or her, over the years, and what didn't happen. The truth is what you said and didn't say, how much you tried, how you changed, and whether you were lucky. I believe in luck. I think luck plays a huge part in success. Or failure. In the end, who cares about the truth? You still end up divorced.

Finally, the biggest asshole wins. Sort of. At least the biggest asshole takes home the most stuff. If you consider this winning, then have at it. You're an asshole.

Chapter Three

OUR TWO DAUGHTERS, Bea and Ruthann, were nineteen and sixteen at the time Stig and I split up. They have suffered, and it has been painful to watch. I have done all I can do to minimize their pain, but in fact I have often made it much, much worse. I think they have learned what not to do. But I doubt I've taught them anything about what they ought to do.

Ruthann called from college a few years ago and said, "Mom, we are women of metaphor." I laughed, but I realized she made a good point.

Imagine this situation: You wake up one morning, married though not happily and yet not willing to do anything about it, and you cannot open your mouth. You think to your brilliant self, Shit. You call your dentist, Smiley, who says, "Take four Motrin, and see what happens." This works the first time. Your mouth opens. You go about your day.

A week later you wake up unable to open your mouth, but this time, all the Motrin in the universe does not help. Smiley sends you to an oral surgeon, Bob, who diagnoses TMJ, or temporomandibular joint syndrome. The oral surgeon, Bob, a short, bald and droll man in scrubs, says to you, "This is usually stress-related, Margaret. You have to get rid of the stress in your life." You vigorously deny having any stress whatsoever, despite the fact that you look and sound like Joan Crawford wearing orthodontic headgear. Bob nods at you in a way that indicates he finds you self-deluded in the extreme and writes you a prescription for physical therapy. After three months of constant pain and liquid meals during which you manage to gain weight, you have gone to physical therapy, a Korean acupuncturist, a yogi from the Bronx, a masseuse specializing in TMJ issues (who knew?), and have purchased all sorts of equipment that allows you to creatively hang various body parts from doorknobs in an effort to achieve complete temporomandibular relaxation. In your quest for said relaxation, you consider the installation of inversion boots over your bathtub, along with optional snorkeling equipment, when you instead choose to have a general anesthetic so that your oral surgeon Bob can forcibly open your joint, flush it out, and give you an injection of steroids. After all these therapies, you are able to fit one small grape into your mouth, but not chew it. And at each visit to your droll oral surgeon, he repeats his mantra, "Margaret, you have to get rid of the stress in your life."

Here's the remarkable thing about the human body and Bob: both are much smarter than I heretofore recognized. A mere three weeks after moving away from my husband, on a glorious summer morning, I, bearing an alarming resemblance to Sleeping Beauty, woke up, sat up, stretched, and yawned! That's right. I yawned. I opened my mouth and yawned! Three weeks after I left home, I woke up one morning and opened my mouth, quite normally. It appears I'd gotten rid of the stress in my life. The stress had a name—it was beside mine on my marriage certificate.

We are women of metaphor.

I assumed there were also men of metaphor. I assumed I would eventually meet some. But now, with my mouth finally and irrevocably open, I had to begin the process of marital decompression.

The early days, the days just after I left, were not easy.

I lived in our weekend house for the summer, waiting for my job to begin, waiting for the Chicago condo to sell. Waiting.

Mostly, I sat on a glider on a screened porch while overlooking a ravine from a home we'd built together in southwestern Michigan and cried.

Rocked, and cried.

Drank wine, and cried.

Talked on the phone, and cried.

Kate and Neal called every day. Hayley and Daniel too. Neal and Daniel wanted to beat up Stig. I told them it wasn't necessary, but thanks.

My mother called every day, and sometimes came to visit on weekends. But I had to be careful. I could not break down in front of her because of her recent bypass surgery, her grief from my dad's death, and her silent shock at the failure of my marriage. My mom had always been my confidante, and I was her rock. But now I felt, perversely, like a burden.

My sister Beth called every day.

"What are you going to do today?" she would ask. Every day. Beth enunciates words very precisely. Our mother taught us that. I rebelled and became the quiet one who mumbles. Beth listened.

"I don't know," I would say, weeping. "I can't think that far in advance."

"But Margaret, in the meantime . . ."

"Don't you love that phrase—in the meantime? As if there's a future?"

My life existed completely in the meantime. I was all mean-time. I suddenly had no future.

I was a mess.

A friend recommended a divorce lawyer. Not that I was plan-ning on filing for divorce, but I realized I needed some advice. I spent two hours in her office telling her an incoherent story, and crying. Her assistant had the whitest teeth I have ever seen in my life. Their translucence nearly blinded me. I may have put on sun-glasses.

For this, she charged me a lot of money. I don't remember any advice she gave me, but I do remember those teeth.

I would recommend, based on this experience, using lawyers more judiciously than I did. Use them to convey numbers and stone cold facts. Anything else is a waste of time and money. They pretend to care, but they are charging you for their time while they affect a pretense of caring. They blind you with their designer teeth. They do not care. They do not give a rat's ass how much you tried, that you really wanted to work it out, that you did all you could. Forget about it! You are wasting money. Good money that you could use to pay rent, or use to feed your children, or to give to a worthwhile charity, or to take a well-deserved vacation.

I recently heard about a guy who had spent $3 million in legal fees over five years and had not seen a single one of his five kids during those five years. Now granted, odds are the guy is a repre-hensible schmuck. But people who pay that much money are fools. Get some decent legal representation.

I came into my divorce with a handful of assumptions. These included the conviction that I was guaranteed vindication as well as my absolute certainty that I would simply move from one marriage into another, or at least into another committed relationship. Because who wants to be alone? Marriage is the goal, right? Not wholeness. Not learning to be healthy alone. Not figuring out what mistakes you made and how not to repeat them. I knew, theoretically, that I had to heal. So fine, I'd heal. I'd go into therapy, shed a few tears for my twenty-year marital error. And then I'd be done. A new man might even help me through all that. I just had to find him. Out with the old, in with the new. Grieve what I'd lost, and move on. But first I had to . . .

Get organized. For me, that meant cleaning out closets, the fridge, drawers. Giving away old clothes. I gave away everything that didn't fit. Done.

Move out. Done.

Get a job. Done. It would start in the fall.

Find therapist. Check.

Find lawyer. Check. Find another lawyer, this time one with normal teeth. Check again.

And file for divorce. Because he filed first. Okay. Check.

But then I had to get through the actual days. Because the days, in the early months—I don't know if it's like this for anyone else—after I left him, after twenty years together, when I had no idea how or why it had ended, when I hadn't yet learned what the narrative would be, I didn't know about the girlfriend, or all the girlfriends rather, all I knew was that he had turned into someone I no longer knew or trusted, I could barely stop crying long enough to steer my car to the liquor store. I took it there quite frequently. I couldn't sleep unless I drank a half a bottle of wine before bed. I cried until my head ached. And I had headaches each and every day.

I read my way through that first summer. I took bike rides with my new divorce lawyer Adam and by myself. My friends Kate and Neal and Hayley and Daniel came to spend weekends with me.

And I read books. Not romances, as if I gave a crap about that stuff anymore, but mysteries. Robert B. Parker had written twenty-nine, as of the summer of 2002, Spenser novels. I decided to read them in the order in which they were written. It was a goal. Everybody needs a goal. It was something I could accomplish in between visits to Adam and my therapist. I collected some books from the used bookstore down the road, ordered the rest from Amazon. Once I had all twenty-nine, I put a piece of masking tape on each book, numbered them in chronological order, and began to read. I started with *The Godwulf Manuscript*, which Parker wrote in 1973. I liked thinking about how the character of Spenser changed over time, about how the relationship between Susan and Hawk developed and how Spenser probably represented Parker's alter ego. Sometimes I watched Robert Urich in the reruns of *Spenser: For Hire*, but he didn't seem tough enough, Avery Brooks seemed too flashy and glib, and Barbara Stock too tepid. I liked the fact that Spenser didn't cheat on Susan, even though they weren't married. Not every man cheated! I decided I wanted to have an affair with Hawk. It did not bother me that he was a fictional character. Even better! As a matter of fact, I would have an affair. It felt like it was my turn. I might like sex if I ever tried it again. If not with Hawk, then with someone just like him. Why not? I'd been a good girl all my life. I married the right guy, from the right family, cooked gourmet meals, made a perfect home, made perfect children, even grew a perfect garden, from seeds, in the basement, under lights, stayed trim and fit, and still it hadn't been enough. I'd made homemade chicken apple sausages, for God's sake. Ground the meat in my grandmother's hand grinder, stuffed it into the casing with an old-fashioned funnel. And I worked full time as a doctor until recently. Plus, I knew how to do the maintenance on all our major appliances. See where all that perfection got me? Alone. At forty-four.

Stig told me he wanted his share of my clothing, in a phone conversation punctuated with yelling. I didn't think I had much that would fit him. And he wanted his share of my jewelry, as though his gifts to me were things he could simply reclaim. He wasn't just threatening to take back twenty years of stuff; he was taking back twenty years of memories and affection. We were at that crazy point, the point of hyperbolic meanness that should be documented on film and shown to everyone who even considers saying "I do." We were competing for the title of Ugly.

When Kate and Neal came for weekends, Neal cooked while Kate put her arms around me and held me while I cried. They brought their dogs. The dogs played with Olga, and Neal made homemade apple pies and chocolate chip cookies and cherry pies and blueberry scones and peach cobbler, and I ate it all. My clothes stopped fitting. And I cried some more.

I was fat. I was depressed. I was out of shape. I was forty-four years old. Was I wallowing in self-pity? I was fucking swimming in it.

"Honey, I know it seems like this part of your life is going to go on forever, but it's not. Things will get better, you'll feel better, you'll meet someone, you will have sex again—"

I burst into tears.

Kate, Neal, and I sat on the screened porch overlooking Lake Michigan one evening in late August, eating burgers and corn salad and fresh tomatoes from the farmer's market. The sun hung low through the trees, and the crickets buzzed. The dogs lay at our feet, alert for morsels of food that might drop their way.

"I'd do you." Neal smiled at me, then looked at Kate.

She smiled back and covered his hand with hers. "So would I. But I won't go down on you. I guess that's why I can't be a lesbian. But I would loan you Neal, cuz it's for a good cause."

"Thanks, guys," I said. They were an unlikely pair, these two. He was wired, edgy, thin, athletic, and she was laid back, warm, someone you wanted to sit beside and cuddle with. We often did. But somehow they made it work and had two wonderful daughters close in age to my own.

"Just don't let the Sperm Donor get to you, honey."

"I never liked him," Neal said. He took a giant bite of his hamburger, chewed, and looked thoughtful. "I thought he was pompous and condescending."

"It's amazing how many people have said something to that effect, now that we're separated." I'd been hearing from friends, family, distant relatives, friends of distant relatives, coworkers, former coworkers, acquaintances, service workers, the maintenance crew at our condo building, and people I hadn't seen in years. Word sure traveled fast. Turned out nobody could stand the guy. Why don't they tell you that before you marry him?

"Do you think he's having an affair?" Kate asked. She pushed the corn salad around her plate. "Is this white balsamic in here?"

"Yes and yes," I said. "I asked him. He said, 'No, are you?' But the kids both told me they think he has a girlfriend."

"Nice." Neal nodded.

"And Ruthann found some cheap makeup in my bathroom at home. So apparently she's leaving her stuff there, spending the night in my bed while my sixteen-year-old daughter is sleeping in the next room. Ruthie hasn't seen her though. He doesn't come home until the middle of the night."

"Cocksucker," Kate said.

"Holy shit." Neal shook his head.

"I know."

"We're here for you, you know that, right?" She covered both my hands with both of hers. "Anything we can do, just let us do it."

"Thanks. I love you guys. If I do decide to have sex with Neal, I'm sure I could get you a tax deduction. Somehow. It would be a charitable contribution on his part."

They both nodded. "We love you."

Chapter Four

SOMEHOW, FORTUITOUSLY, IN a few brief weeks over the summer, the condo sold. I'd done some preliminary research with a Realtor, and when the girls came back from their trips, Bea and Ruthann and I looked at real estate together. Finally I took them to see a small unit in a vintage condo a few blocks away from our old building. *Vintage* in Chicago means doormen, high assessments, and no parking. But the building allowed dogs, had good security, and we agreed it felt like a home. Ruthie wouldn't have to leave her carpool. I found parking next door. The condo was dark and dismal, a cave, albeit a sophisticated one. But it felt finished, and we could move right in. We had a sense it wouldn't be permanent.

I saw Stig only once in late August, when I moved back from Michigan so that Ruthie could start her junior year and Bea could go back to Kenyon. I had to pack up our Chicago apartment.

Shortly before the move I stood in the kitchen, going through screwdrivers and Christmas lights and vacuum cleaners. I put aside the ice-cream maker for the building engineer. His name was Carlo. It was a gift I'd never taken out of the box. I thought Carlo deserved at least an ice-cream maker for telling me why my marriage was over.

Stig had put little mauve Post-it Notes on the things he wanted—furniture, artwork, rugs, mirrors, lamps. The whole apartment was covered with these Post-it Notes. It seemed like he wanted everything, but the notes kept falling off and landing on the floor. The kids were horrified.

"So you're taking the hot glue gun."

He'd come up behind me, silently, holding the box. I turned around and put down the packing tape in my hand.

"Yes," I answered. "I'm taking the hot glue gun. Did you want it?"

"No. I just wanted to point out that you're taking it."

I raised my eyebrows.

"It's fine," he said. "I can always get another one."

I left behind a lot of stuff when I left my husband. My wedding dishes, crystal, everyday dishes, pots and pans, silverware. My CDs. Most of the family photos. Some Christmas decorations. Even my skis.

One day while packing, I threw out all my lingerie. Every single piece, except underwear I'd bought at the Gap. I regretted this later. Anyway, I left him the toaster, the microwave, the colander. I took the electric drill but left the electric screwdriver. I'm sure that was a sublimation of something, but I don't know what.

On Friday the thirteenth, September 2002, shortly after Bea rushed away to her second year at college, Ruthann and I moved into a two-bedroom with no view, high ceilings, large rooms, a working fireplace, and an eat-in kitchen. One nice thing about vintage is that the walls and floors are thick, and your privacy is ensured. You can cry hard in the middle of the night, and no one hears. The neighbors keep to themselves, for the most part, but they will stop and chat at the mailboxes or the garbage cans or the gas-powered grills in the courtyard on occasion. The previous owner had painted everything a dull, dark beige, which matched my mood and outlook. We felt we were moving into a bomb shelter, going into hiding, hunkering down, awaiting the all clear. This was our second move in less than three years and we had nothing extraneous remaining in our lives.

While the movers set up furniture, I sent Ruthie to Bed Bath & Beyond with a credit card and a list. She spent hundreds of dollars on utensils and housewares both on and not on the list. She bought us a wok. Later we ordered silverware online, then used plastic for eight weeks until it arrived. We bought French posters for our kitchen, and a clock with the Eiffel tower stenciled in black. We hung pictures, ate peanut butter and jelly for dinner, and slept together for the first six weeks. She forced me to exercise when all I wanted to do was sleep, and I forced her to go to school when she was so depressed she wanted to stay home. She held me when I cried, and I rubbed her back on the days she saw her father and sobbed about how he'd changed.

One Sunday morning every October the marathon goes past our building, and the neighbors stand together in the chill air, searching the crowd for familiar faces, talking about our bad knees, thinking about how life chips away at our potential, athletic as well as otherwise, and defines the roads not taken. Or at least that's what I think about. Watching 45,000 people run past makes you a little seasick from lateral nystagmus, the way the eyes naturally move back and forth, so you must change tactics now and then. Clap your hands, jump up and down, face different directions.

But on Friday the thirteenth of September, after a day of moving, the phone rang.

"Margaret?" The voice was deep and melodious, and I did not recognize it.

"Yes, this is Margaret."

"Margaret, this is Leo. Leo Kennedy."

Leo Kennedy had been a prominent Chicago ad exec and a friend of my former brother-in-law. I'd known his ex-wife, Annalisa. Now he was retired. I recalled him as a proper, dignified man who had once broken both legs while skydiving. That's how I remember people—by their medical problems. I hadn't seen him in years. Why would he be calling me?

"Margaret, I'm so glad to be able to speak with you. I've been wanting to call for months, ever since I heard you were separated."

Really? I wondered why. I'm dense sometimes. Then I tried to figure out how old he was.

"I'd like to take you to dinner." He was twenty-six years older than Annalisa, who was about four years older than me. How old did that make him?

He wanted to ask me out for dinner? Was he crazy? He was at least seventy! Maybe older!

"Um, oh, uh, Leo, I don't think so." Pure panic had set in. I didn't recognize it at first.

To be fair, I have older friends. I often eat with them. I am not ageist. But this didn't feel like an older friend thing. And besides that, I never really liked the guy. Because—because—

"What are you worried about? Are you worried about Annal-isa? I run into Annalisa all the time. I'm sure she wouldn't mind."

Was he asking me out on a date? It sounded suspiciously like a date. *Eeeeuw.* The thought of dating a friend's ex had never oc-curred to me. The thought of dating anyone specific had never occurred to me. When I thought of dating, I thought of it in the generic sense, imagined, on the page, at a distance. Not with a real honest-to-goodness person attached. But now that I thought about it, my reaction was . . . not a seventy-year-old. I kept trying to add, or subtract, whatever the proper function was. Algebra? Trigonometry? I was forty-four. That made him—seventy-three? Seventy-four? Normally I was very good at math. I'd been an Illinois State Math Scholar in high school. And a National Merit Finalist. I'd been accepted to Stanford, for God's sake. This was not a quadratic equation. But for some reason, my mind had gone blank. All I knew was this proposal was not a mathematical possibility. It felt wrong. Now I had to find the proof.

"Well, there's that," I said. "But Leo, it's just too soon for me. Really, I'm not ready yet." Like, for example, I still cried every day. Or just call it sobbing. Self-flagellation in the form of how-did-I-fuck-up-my-own-life-for-so-long hours of sobbing, performed ritualistically, on a daily basis. Some people might see that as a deterrent to dating, only in the sense that I might not be a rip-snorting good time. I could barely get to the grocery store without a box of Kleenex. I mean—I was with Stig for twenty-three years and married to him for twenty of them. We'd been separated three months. So some people would recognize that I wasn't ready. Hell, I was reading books with numbered pieces of masking tape on the side, fantasizing about an actor named Avery Brooks, and analyz-ing the casting choices of a fifteen-year-old detective TV show!

But not Leo. Not that he knew of my feelings for Avery, but still.

"That's okay, I'll wait. So what do you think? Maybe a week, two weeks? I'll wait three weeks, then call? What do you think? Three weeks?"

I suppose at seventy-four, Leo didn't have a lot of time to waste.

"Oh, Leo, I don't think so. I mean, I have no idea when I'll want to date, but even then, I mean, you're . . . well . . . you're not . . ." I didn't want to say—you probably won't be alive then.

"Margaret, I've admired you for years. Even when I was married to Annalisa, I remember thinking—"

All I could think was . . . *eeeeeuw*. I wanted to put this gently, but Leo seemed immune to gentle.

"Leo! You're too old for me!"

"Nonsense, Margaret. Age is a state of mind. Mind over matter. If you don't mind, it doesn't matter."

"Oh, Leo, I do mind. And it matters. Thanks for your call."

"Tell you what . . . I'll give you a call in another week. We'll see how you're feeling. I won't go away, Margaret. I really want to see you. We don't have to have dinner—we can have a drink. I'll buy."

"Thanks, Leo. I have to go—oops, another call. Take care!"

I let Leo go to voicemail for the next couple of weeks, but I registered the wake-up call. Does anyone plan on being single at forty-four? I'd avoided my reflection for a decade. Perhaps I should take stock of the goods. One night I took off all my clothes and stood in front of a full-length mirror. The overhead lighting accentuated my cellulite and wrinkles, made me look depressed, and just a wee bit criminally insane. I noted I was plump. When it happens gradually, over years, your eyes accommodate to the view. I turned to the side. At least I had boobs now. I seemed fluffed up, but the fluffing hadn't happened . . . symmetrically. I'd poofed up and out of shape. I wondered—where exactly had my waistline gone? Was this a permanent situation? Could I ever get it back? And since when did my ass blend into my upper thighs? I weighed—yikes!— what I'd weighed when I delivered Ruthie.

I looked like a woman who'd been left in middle age, even if I had done the leaving, technically. I had to keep reminding myself of that. I might be attractive to a seventy-four-year-old, but this was not necessarily a good thing. I'd always liked clothes, and I spent a fair amount of money on my wardrobe, but in the previous several years I'd allowed it to become Eileen Fisher-esque, meaning I had elastic in most if not all waistbands and a lot of flat shoes in the closet. I'd worked in an operating room for twenty-plus years, which saves money on work-related clothing. Certainly nothing beats scrubs for comfort. While I didn't think that my clothing had anything to do with the failure of my marriage, I realized, in retrospect, I had allowed a certain frumpiness to take over my life.

My divorce lawyer, Adam, told me to go out and buy some new clothes. What did that mean? Did I look that bad? In fact, he made it sound kind of deductible. I'd be starting to date again, he told me. Okay. When did that happen? I believed him, though I wasn't too sure how to go about meeting men.

Then one Saturday afternoon I was on the Internet, shopping for things I didn't need, for hobbies I didn't have but was convinced I should cultivate. I would begin with cake decorating. But I needed the proper equipment. I found a Web site and started clicking away—pastry bags, cake wheel, box of tips, or should I buy them individually? Did I want the box of 12, 24, 48, or would I just go ahead and buy all 128 pastry tips? Cheaper shipping! Plus the brushes to clean—I couldn't decide between reusable bags and disposable. I spent forever deliberating. Pretty soon my shopping cart was up to $700, and I couldn't wait to get started! I longed to learn the basket-weave pattern. But then I wondered, who is going to eat this cake? I knew nothing about cake decorating. I'd like to learn, but . . . maybe I should take a class first. I started to delete and kept deleting until the shopping cart was empty.

Then a screen popped up. Match.com. I followed the link. And I was instantly mesmerized. I typed in my zip code, the age range—men forty to fifty. Within ten miles of my zip code. And I pressed a button. And up popped twenty (yes, twenty) pages of men. It was like the Home Shopping Network, only better—a weirdly attractive combination of shopping, Modern Romance, and voyeurism, without any calories or shipping charges.

I did not know how to meet men, nor did I know anything about them, but I thought meeting men was something I ought to do. I liked male companionship. I was not bitter about my divorce, yet. Maybe if I met a nice guy, I wouldn't cry so much. But I needed practice. I didn't go to bars, I was paralyzed with shyness, and almost all my friends were married or gay. The Internet seemed like a good place to start.

I read for days. I read the profiles. I believed every word I read. I found it all fascinating—the format, the combination of multiple choice and freeform expressions of individuality, the stated hobbies and interests, the way the men seemed to know exactly what they were looking for in a woman. I saw each profile as a story—a story purporting to tell the world who this person was, in his own words. And because I am the world's most gullible individual, it never occurred to me that people might be married, or lying.

All I knew was that I didn't want my husband. As I read through profiles, I recognized some very angry people. They sounded like me, actually, or like the me I didn't want to acknowledge. I would have to be careful.

Some of these men showed pictures more suitable to the post office than an Internet dating site. They looked scary. Some showed themselves wearing hats that took ten points right off the tops of their IQs, or wearing wedding rings, or with their arms around women who looked suspiciously like wives or who had been incompletely cut out of the picture. But occasionally a man appeared . . . not bad, and some were downright attractive. After a week I wanted to respond. But my elderly Web browser couldn't accommodate me. I couldn't figure out how to upload, download, or save. I didn't have a picture of myself. I couldn't find the digital camera. When I found it, I tried to take my own picture, but I looked depressed, distorted. These were fairly accurate representations of me, but not what I wanted to show to the world. I asked my daughter to take my picture. Then I wondered, *What am I doing?*

Ruthann came into my room one evening, watching as I read profile after profile.

"Mom, you might actually have to leave the apartment if you want to find a date."

"I don't think so," I answered. "With the Internet, I can have a complete relationship without leaving the comfort of my own home."

She rolled her eyes.

I figured it out eventually. Ruthie took a picture that wasn't too terrible, I spent a week or so trying to go about uploading it, then another week filling out my own profile. And voila! I was on the Internet and ready to date.

On a Thursday evening in November 2002, AOL weather said the temperature was twenty-four degrees Fahrenheit in Chicago. I live near Lake Michigan—which theoretically acts as a repository of heat in the winter so that it is "warmer near the lake." In the summer it is "cooler near the lake." The problem is that it is also windy along the lakefront, so the temperature in winter turns out to feel the same as it is away from the lake—that is, cold.

The date was a last-minute thing. My first date in twenty-three years, since 1979 to be exact, and I barely had time to get ready.

Twenty-three years turned out to be a long time to go between dates. It was a long time to have let one's social skills slide, as it were. During that period I'd gone to med school, gotten married, had two daughters, done an anesthesiology residency, practiced anesthesia, cooked a lot of fancy meals, eaten tons of bad hospital food, broken some bones, torn some ligaments, dislocated an ankle, planted some gardens, learned flower arranging and decorating, read lots of books, and buried my dad. I'd had motion sickness (cars, planes, and boats), food poisoning, salmonella, sun poisoning, poison oak, poison ivy, and I'd developed hives on my only two trips to the Caribbean. In other news, the Berlin Wall had fallen. The USSR had dissolved. Poverty had continued unabated. George W. Bush had somehow become president of the US of A. Nine-eleven had demolished our impregnable mentality, our national sense of safety, and for some of us, our individual sense of safety. The world had changed completely. I felt as though the kids were my major accomplishment, but the question of accomplishment was one that plagued me regularly—on New Year's and birthdays in particular.

I'd spent years overachieving in the hopes that my husband would want to come home if I made everything just *perfect*, and now I had a lot of skills and no husband. All in all, what had I really accomplished? Divorce seems to infect the very roots of our self-esteem.

Anyway—I started slow on Match.com. A hesitant letter here. A few men sent me e-mails. Some I answered. I didn't have any stringent set of criteria regarding which I answered and which I didn't, but that didn't bother me. I had no idea what I was doing, and I was pretty clear on that. I engaged in an exchange with a optometrist from the northwest side who stressed Catholicism as a way to improve my life. I didn't write back. Some conversations were ended by me, and some by the guy. Anyone with even a passing resemblance to Stig, I immediately deleted. And then there was an e-mail from Ed, who stated that he was a doctor. Perfect! Another doctor seemed just the thing for me, because I hadn't learned my lesson the first time. Ed and I e-mailed for a couple of weeks, but that was okay. E-mail exchanges alone gave me heart palpitations, so I knew not to rush into anything. But I thought— the way most people who are leaving long marriages think—that I would probably find my soul mate within a month or two, then live happily ever after.

Ed—we'll call him Ed to save on space—was a doctor of psychology. This was important to me because, as a physician, I thought it appropriate to date men as educated as myself. This was not exactly total snobbishness on my part, more a shorthand way of trying to find a man whose intellectual curiosity equaled mine. There's no box to check for that on Match.com.

Okay, fine, I am a snob. But luckily, there's no specific box for that either.

So . . . Ed and I exchanged photos. I thought he looked okay.

He thought I was gorgeous. This earned him some points. Not long after declaring me gorgeous, Ed asked me out on a date. For that same evening. Not knowing any better, I said yes. I had four hours to get ready. It was long enough to get really nervous, but not long enough to lose twenty pounds.

So here's how I went about getting myself ready. Because I immediately became an anxious wreck, I cleaned the entire house, even cleaned out a few drawers in the fridge. There were some old tomatoes, some icky lettuce; they definitely had to be thrown away before I could even consider going on a date. Then I took Olga for a long walk. Next I took a shower, tried on six outfits, settled on the least sexy thing I owned (think thick nubbly sweater with a very high neck), talked to two encouraging sisters on the phone, and decided to walk to the bar where we were going to meet. Which was fourteen blocks away. The temperature now hovered at twenty-one degrees, with a brisk wind. Do I sound like a wimp? I'm not really a wimp. Anyway—I stopped walking three times, shouted out loud to myself, "What are you doing? You're such an asshole!", turned around, called myself "Coward!", then turned back. This went on for a few blocks—"Asshole! Coward!"—but eventually I arrived at my destination. I entered the bar. And Ed was there. I'd thought he might stand me up.

Ed looked a lot like the picture, though maybe not quite so good. Short gray hair, close to bald, short gray goatee. Excellent nose. He was medium height, well dressed, and a little awkward, like someone who is not athletic and has never quite come to terms with it. I caught a glimpse of myself in the bar mirror—bright red, flushed cheeks, sweaty nose. I resembled a woman in the throes of a hot flash. Which, in fact, I was. Despite being frozen solid.

We sat at the bar. He had a glass of wine. I ordered a glass of wine.

"Tell me about your research," I said to Ed the psychologist.

"I study sexual behavior," Ed answered.

"Ah," I said, nodding. Of course he did.

Ed explained the reason why women fall in love with men after having sex, and why men don't, because they're chemically hunter-gatherers. Or something. I quickly lost track of the explanation due to its blatant absurdity.

He suggested we move from the bar to the back room, where there was a fireplace with comfy chairs gathered around. And we talked more, and easily. The thing that I know about me is that I can talk to almost anybody about almost anything—for a while at least. Here are some of the things I noticed.

I noticed that I remembered everything he said and I said in our e-mails. He did not. Clearly I was obsessive compulsive and he was not, or he was having multiple e-mail conversations with multiple women while I was having one, with him.

He brought up his divorce right away, said he felt guilty about this and guilty about that. While this was all very interesting, I wondered about why he needed to declare his guilt so soon, right up front. I didn't feel guilty about my divorce. I waited too long, if anything. So what was that about?

I wondered if his declaration of guilt meant he cheated on his wife. That would be bad.

We talked about his work, my work. I asked what I thought of as intelligent questions. He gave some intelligent answers. However, he seemed particularly uninterested in my intelligence. That's never a good sign—it's pretty much my major attribute. We knew a few of the same people. He'd dated a surgeon I once worked with. Our talk was relatively serious, in contrast to our e-mails, which were fun and funny. In person, his sense of humor seemed limited by his . . . person.

It occurred to me more than once that he was checking out the other women in the place, while we were talking. This did not bother me, though I couldn't tell you why. But it did not earn him any points either. The place filled up around us, but because I was sitting with my back to the door, I didn't really notice except that the noise level gradually built.

Then he said, "I can hardly hear you," and he climbed into my chair with me. While it was an oversize chair, it was still a chair. It was not a loveseat, not a double chair, not a couch. It was designed for one person. And we now had two people sitting in it. He looked very silly, running his hand through my hair, squished sideways into my chair.

In retrospect, I could only imagine the look on my face, but I'm guessing it was something like abject horror. I did not say a word. Apparently, I didn't have to.

He asked, "Am I making you uncomfortable?"

"Yes," I said, "you are."

He looked at me as though I had the problem, then vacated my chair with alacrity, and we continued our conversation as if the chair-squishing incident had never occurred. Then he suavely asked for the check.

Once outside, he offered me a ride home, saying, "Don't worry, I won't pounce, unless you want me to." He may have wiggled an eyebrow.

Eeeeeuw.

I took the proffered ride, because I was relatively certain I could handle a pouncing psychologist (I'd been working out) and because it was really cold. Probably closer to sixteen degrees.

Inside the car, I noticed dead leaves on the floorboard that crack-led beneath my feet. Could this be a symbol—they were dead—and my life was over? Or maybe something else? Something autumnal, perhaps, a comment on my age, lack of ripeness . . . Or forget sym-bols. Were they simply a sign? I should make like a tree and—? I pulled myself back from the leaf motif.

Our conversation took on a serious tone. "So how does this work," I asked, "this dating thing?" But I was really asking about sex, and he understood that, even if I didn't.

"Well," he hesitated, "do you want me to be perfectly honest?"

"Yes." No, we're having this conversation so that you can lie to me. Don't you wonder about people who ask if you want them to be perfectly honest? As if they lie to you by default except when you give your express permission for them to be perfectly honest?

"I've dated a lot of women. And what usually happens is, after a month of sleeping together, I find a way to extricate myself from the relationship. And it's painful. Because even if the woman says she's just interested in something casual, she gets hurt. I think a woman's interest in a man grows once they're sleeping together, whereas a man stays interested for about a month, then he stops. There's actually hormonal evidence to substantiate this scenario." He paused. "Am I shocking you?"

I was thinking about a *Seinfeld* episode that essentially said the same thing, only it was funnier. Now I felt horrified and a little sick. Is this what life had in store for me? Is this what it meant to be single at forty-four, or fifty, or fifty-five? Bozos like Ed who just wanted to get laid? Why date a doctor if you only want one month of sex? It would take me that long to get past the germ issues!

"No," I calmly answered, though I was shivering and clutching my sleeves. This guy, sitting beside me, was every woman's worst nightmare. He was using scientific research and probably U.S. government grant money to justify being a jerk!

"Should I turn the heat up?"

"Hmm. I wish I had my notebook. I like to write everything down."

He turned his head and looked at me. We were at a stoplight, so this was safer than it sounds.

"I mean, I can masturbate. I'm sure you masturbate. And I'm really looking for a nice woman to settle down with, someone I can love and be comfortable with and spend the rest of my life with."

Yeah, right, I thought. The rest of his life, or a month, whichever came first.

"What about fun?" I asked, as we pulled up to the side of my building.

Ed turned toward me and stretched his arm out behind my seat. "Fun is important. But—I don't know—maybe fun can help us get beyond the month. Fun helps. Sometimes I think it helps to get sex out of the way first. We could do that tonight, if you like. Just get it out of the way." He looked hopeful and innocent. Or rather, he looked like a caricature of innocence. Did that work with some women? The idiot subset?

"Thanks, but I'm fine," I answered, thinking that in some important ways absolutely nothing had changed since 1979. Only now I was older. More vulnerable.

Then he moved closer, and I realized he was going to kiss me. Time slowed down, and his nose loomed impossibly large. I stared at it, eyes slowly crossing. He smelled pretty good. It didn't occur to me to close my eyes. I decided to let him kiss me, because it had been twenty-three years since I'd kissed anyone other than Stig, and I thought maybe I should practice in case someone I actually wanted to kiss were to come along. So Ed kissed me, and it did not make me want to hurl, which seemed like a good outcome, overall. I am a scientist, and I believe in experimentation.

During the course of this kiss, which was open-mouthed but not sloppy, I noticed other parts of me sluggishly coming to life.

I thought, *I am not dead.*

Yay!

I might not be exactly alive, but I was not completely dead either. Then I extricated my mouth and said to Ed the psychologist, "I'm outta here."

Chapter Five

IN THE LATE fall of 2002, I got busy with divorce paperwork that seemed unending. I also had a new job to prepare for, a new condo to turn into a home, some weight to shed, nearly constant headaches, and a self-image that, never good, now circled the drain as my husband's girlfriend grew from suspicion into grim reality. And so, like any middle-aged woman or man suffering from debilitating loss and/or rejection, I embarked on a frenzied phase of Internet dating. Because . . . it was there. Because I could. It's not as though you need a license.

Following my aborted chair rendezvous with Ed the psychologist, I met Angel, a banker, who arrived twenty minutes late at a local coffee shop.

I was on my way out the door when Angel hurried in. He appeared sweaty and disheveled, his face covered with tiny lacerations. I found the ground-meat look instantly riveting, in a purely dark, clinical way. He was tall and not unattractive, though he looked like he had been shaved by a Weimaraner with a straight blade.

"I'm parked illegally," Angel told me, eyes darting, as if parking were not all he had done illegally. "Do you mind accompanying me to my car?" I could not control my fascination with his cut-up face, and his obvious anxiety. The doctor in me went along. Didn't think twice. We drove to Lincoln Park where we walked through the Zoo.

"I have a confession," Angel said. Of course he did. Outdoors he seemed more relaxed and unguarded, and I am someone people always confess to. I am priestlike in that sense, but without the vestments, the cute little cubby, the privacy screen, the Hail Marys. Total and near-total strangers tell me their most intimate thoughts, wishes, histories, details. Sometimes they walk right up on the street and start telling me about relationships gone awry. I wish they didn't. The worst environment for me is an airplane, particularly first class. Get a drink or two in people, and they really unload. I've taken to bringing headphones, wearing dark glasses, and reading a newspaper, all at the same time. "I wrote to you earlier in the fall under an alias, using a different picture, wearing a goatee. It was a different name and profile."

Still new to the Internet dating scene, I nodded but withheld judgment.

I glanced at him. Angel wore nice enough clothes—a black leather jacket, black slacks, and a mock turtleneck sweater—but I admit it struck me as odd to hear him use the word *alias* when describing his dating activities. I gripped my hands together and stared at the frolicking sea otters.

"Why?" I asked.

"I like trying out different personas, seeing what types of women I can attract. Do you remember? We had had a discussion about your grocery store, the Dominick's on Broadway. I told you I'd seen cockroaches in the produce section. I don't think you wrote back after that."

"Oh, yeah. Now I remember. I still shop there."

We walked to the Conservatory, my favorite place in Lincoln Park.

"I have obsessive-compulsive disorder," he said, as we entered the orchid room. Normally I love this room, but Angel was looking pretty pale and chopped up, so it seemed best not to linger.

"The reason I have so many cuts on my face is because I shaved six times before I came to meet you."

I nodded. "Huh," I said.

We studied the epiphytes.

"Would you like to have dinner?" Angel asked.

"Um, sure," I answered. "I guess. We both have to eat, right?"

We stopped and sat down on a bench along the path that wound through the Conservatory. I felt him staring at me.

"What?" I asked.

"You look like a movie star," he told me.

I laughed. "Yeah, right."

"You know which one."

"Uh, I have no idea what you're talking about. No one has ever told me I look like a movie star before."

"Oh, come on. You know who you look like," Angel said.

"I swear to you, I have no idea who you are referring to. I don't think I look like anyone. Who do you think I look like?"

"It's so obvious. Ashley Judd. No one has ever told you that?"

I think it is fairly safe to say I look nothing like Ashley Judd.

"Um, no. You're the first. But thank you. That's a nice compliment."

Hank, a securities analyst, took *nondescript* and made it a superlative. We met at a diner in my neighborhood.

"On my last date, the woman brought me cookies individually wrapped in cellophane held together with pictures of herself that had been made into tiny little stickers. They were plastered everywhere. She stuck one on my hand when we met. But in comparison, you seem real normal." The lunch went reasonably well, and Hank was dull but showed no obvious signs of self-mutilation, so we decided we'd have dinner the next night. But that evening he called and said he'd been fired from his job.

"Can I make dinner for you?" I offered, feeling terrible for this man I had just met. I invited a total stranger to my apartment. Yes, I did. I did not know this man at all, and I invited him into my home.

Of course he accepted.

Ruthann was not home. I overcooked the Hungarian beef paprikash. Hank was understandably despondent. I couldn't blame him. Besides being fired, he told me about his prostate troubles (benign hypertrophy, he'd had the microwave therapy twice, didn't work the first time), gastrointestinal difficulties (irritable bowel but for a long time indistinguishable from ulcerative colitis), and recent gum surgery (which he was still paying for). His ex-wife had left him for another man. And wasn't paying her share of the child support. The kids lived with him.

It was like having dinner with Eeyore, if Eeyore had been constipated, couldn't pee, and had gingivitis. By the end of the evening, I was ready to leave him too.

Although Nikolaos lived in the same town as my work, we initially met at a Starbucks midway between our two homes. While I was not attracted to him (he looked like a cross between Bill Cosby and

Adolf Hitler), he had a Ph.D. in economics, and relative to the other men I'd met, he had passable manners, some conversational dexterity, and a modest sense of humor. Looking back on this now, I understand why I met him once. But why I went out on four subsequent dates with him—well . . . I know there must have been a reason. Other than the fact that I was crazy, desperate, despondent, and had completely taken leave of my senses. Or maybe those reasons are enough.

Maybe it's because he didn't mention his prostate, his bowels, a hernia, or his propensity to dump women after a month while we drank vanilla lattes.

On the other hand, I should have paid attention when he told me that his wife hid all the hammers in the house when she told him she wanted a divorce.

He was completely unattractive, and I was completely horny. It was a perfect storm.

On our fourth date, we ate dinner in a shopping mall and went to Bloomingdales. I needed some Christmas gifts.

"What kind of cologne are you wearing?" he asked, as we wandered through the scarf section.

"Chanel Allure," I answered.

He brought the tester over, asked if this was it. I said yes, then he sprayed it on me. I sneezed.

He leaned forward and smelled my neck. I remember this specifically because I looked down and noticed his green pants. It's my personal feeling that green pants are almost always a mistake, under any circumstances. I'm not talking khaki, I'm talking green. Then he went and bought me a bottle of the same cologne, which was nice, I guess, but in a weird ingratiating way. I already owned the cologne. This unprovoked act of generosity made me very un-comfortable. I should have paid attention to my instincts, but I'd ignored them for years. They were rust-laden.

This might be a good time to mention a date I had back in sophomore year of high school, shortly after my braces came off.

The president of the student council, a not-unattractive geekoid named Tom, had asked me out. He arrived for our date wearing a striped shirt and plaid pants, which were not green, to his credit. I don't remember much about the date, although I think he took me to see the Village People, and I told him I had to go home early.

"I have to practice my typing," I said, one geekoid to another.

Now while I'm certain that this young student council presi-dent ultimately went far in life, I am just as certain that at some point along the way someone took him aside and advised him about his wardrobe malfeasance. I certainly hope so. Wherever you are, young man, or sir, I apologize. I'm sure you were wonderful. You were, after all, only seventeen.

Nikolaos, on the other hand, was fifty-something and had no excuse.

On our fifth date we went to a movie in his town, ate dinner, then walked to his house. I sat on the sofa in his family room. He told me he had painted his house that day.

I glanced around and sniffed. "Really? The whole thing?"

"Yes, I painted the whole first floor. Today."

A deep bilious green covered the walls, the color you might find in a cheap hotel room, where Norman Bates might live. Nothing was out of place. It didn't smell like fresh paint. It was at this point that I should have gotten up, retrieved my coat, and headed for the door. But common sense had fled.

Nikolaos sat beside me on the couch, put his arm around me, and kissed me, gently. I felt passive, slightly queasy, a little headachy, like just before you get a bad case of the flu. I knew a seduction scene was being played out here. But I decided to go along with it. If someone found me attractive, maybe I would believe in myself again. Even if this someone was a weird creepy guy who looked like Adolf Hitler. I imagined myself having a minor role in a bad sixties movie in which John Astin was putting the moves on me. Slimy. The more obvious Nikolaos was, the less I liked him. It occurred to me that I might be willing to date a duck-billed platypus if it read the *New York Times*, but oddly, Nikolaos did not read the *New York Times*. He said he read fiction and watched Fox News. I glanced around. There were no books or newspapers anywhere to be seen. So clearly I'd opted for an illiterate platypus.

"Would you like to dance?" Nikolaos asked.

"No."

"Come on, just one dance."

"Fine."

So we danced slow, which was, I think, Nikolaos's idea of romance, since he certainly didn't have any rhythm. I thought he seemed like the biggest dork I'd ever met, and you know, in medicine, we work with some of the biggest dorks in the universe. But this guy had real dork moves, let me tell you. I'd seriously begun to regret this date.

And at some point during the evening I realized he'd lied about his age. The numbers didn't add up. The year he'd graduated, the age at which he'd married, the ages of his kids, how long he'd been married. I kept asking questions, trying to do the math in my head. But the numbers didn't make sense. I had a feeling he was eight to ten years older than the age posted on his Match.com profile.

Anyway, we sat down on the couch again, and he stuck his

tongue in my ear. I felt a wave of nausea. Then he said, "I have a present for you."

I distinctly remember thinking to myself, *Oh God, whatever it is, it will be very, very bad.*

He reached under the sofa and whipped out a Victoria's Secret box.

I closed my eyes and may have groaned out loud.

Okay, men—here's the 411 for all you guys who think women get turned on by a gift from Victoria's Secret. Save your money! You wear your dick on your sleeve. There is no greater turnoff. If you want to get laid, let it be her idea. Figure it out. Anyway—back to the story and Mr. Pathetic.

I opened the box, and an acute sense of foreboding filled me. Inside the box sat a green silk teddy. I mean, what was it with this guy and green?

"Wow," I said, shaking my head. "You really shouldn't have."

Then he said, "Why don't you go upstairs and put that on? I'll be up in three minutes."

So. I. Did. I went upstairs. I went into the master bedroom, and the whole time I kept thinking, *What am I doing? What is the matter with me?* But I did it anyway. And I put on a green silk teddy. I mean, women never buy this crap for themselves—I never sleep in silk—it makes my hot flashes terrible. But I sat on his bed, with its surprisingly green bedspread, and watched as Nikolaos, the least appealing man in the solar system, lit about a hundred candles and put Ravel's "Bolero" on the stereo, straight out of the movie *10* because that's how original he was. This seduction scene was so premeditated and sophomoric and just plain yucky that I actually looked around for hidden cameras as well as a fire extinguisher. You know when you teeter on the verge of hysteria? That's where I teetered.

It's not a good place to teeter, sexually or otherwise. Then he started to take off his clothes. And he did a dance. Wiggling his hips around, as if he had rhythm . . . or a Hula Hoop . . . Oh my God . . . Then he ripped off his shirt—buttons went flying, one whacked me on the forearm—and the entire time I struggled to maintain control of my facial features. It was like a horror show in 3D. But fascinating, too. At one point I think I hid my face behind my hands and peeked through my fingers, because it was just as scary as watching *Jurassic Park*! And who knew they manufactured green plaid thongs for men?

Then he turned away, and when he turned back, he was naked, except for this leather thing wrapped around his dick! I stared at it, kind of interested, like you'd stare at a cool insect. I've always liked insects, incidentally, and wanted to be an entomologist as a kid, but I have never, in my entire life (now grant you I was not very experienced, but I am a doctor, and I read widely), seen anything like this leather contraption he had on his wanker, which looked like chaps, you know, but way smaller, and then he started talking about erectile dysfunction and Viagra and why he didn't eat much at dinner and GI absorption and yanking on his pecker and I just stared at him in the flickering candlelight.

When he tried to pull my knees apart and put his head between them, I realized that was the last thing I wanted—what I wanted was to be home with a glass of wine and a good book, or even a bad book! Or just the *New York Times*! The *New Yorker*! That's it! I hadn't read this week's *New Yorker*! Gotta go! I mean, I was nearly hysterical, seriously dyspeptic, disgusted with myself for having gotten into this situation, pissed at him for being a total conniving creep, pissed at myself for not having the sense that God gave me, you name it. Anyway, I told him I had to leave. I muttered something about practicing my typing. I jumped up, ran to the bathroom, threw the teddy on the floor, put on my clothes, ran out the door, and drove home.

The next morning . . .

I received an e-mail from Nikolaos, telling me he loved me.

I kid you not.

I wrote him back, saying I never wanted to see him again.

He wrote me back and said he needed to be with a woman who climaxed more easily.

I was in agreement. Completely. Absolutely. One hundred percent. Good luck and God bless.

I am not making this up.

Here's the thing. I was a disaster. I know that now. And yet I kept going out there, meeting man after man, trying to make everyone like me, using no judgment whatsoever, in the hope that someone would want me again.

People going through a divorce are crazy. Some people—with or without a divorce—are simply crazy all the time. This is an important—and difficult—distinction to make.

Chapter Six

RUTHANN, SIXTEEN at the time, took over reading the Match.com profiles, theorizing that I repeatedly chose pathetic losers and that she could do better. So she came upon a profile of a tall, dark, and handsome man named Brad in early February 2003 and wrote him a letter from me. My depression and extreme lethargy allowed this.

Brad responded, and we met for a drink.

He wore nice cologne.

Clean-shaven and tanned, with a deep, sexy voice and a full head of salt-and-pepper hair, Brad sold something or other. He said it hadn't been going too well. But he smiled when he said it. He had beautiful teeth.

He seemed normal, like a regular guy. Nice, kind. Maybe not Ph.D. material, but regular.

My friend Alan says he's stopped dating women who wear perfume. He says that he's been fooled too many times by artificial scents that cover up their natural pheromones, so it takes him too damned long to figure out whether they are actually compatible. Alan, I think, may have issues, or a really good point.

Brad told me a few things about himself. Married a few times. Very good golfer. No kids. Hadn't finished college. Wasn't from around here. Didn't read much.

It was sexual attraction, pure and simple. Right? No other explanation for it. All I could think about was having sex with this man. It was hard to imagine anyone more wrong for me. But when you are lonely, and horny, and sad, and rejected, you can convince yourself of almost anything.

It's not as though I recognized this right away. I didn't say to myself, *I'll just have sex with this man and be done with it.* Of course not. I thought, *I will have a real relationship with him. Introduce him to my friends and family and the people I work with.* This would justify the sex. Somehow.

Crazy.

Over the course of the winter of 2002–3, headaches came nearly every day, which I attributed to the stress of my divorce. Every week, it seemed, someone would tell me about another one of Stig's infidelities.

"You know, I saw him with a woman . . . I wasn't sure if I should say anything," Adele, a scrub tech, mentioned to me while I washed my hands at the sink outside an operating room.

People I worked with, people he worked with, people I ran into at the grocery store mentioned random women they'd seen with him. Even Janina, my cleaning lady, asked if he was now openly dating the neighbor.

"Janina, what neighbor?" I asked. I hadn't heard about this one.

"You know, that woman who so in love with him. The one down

the block at your old house. She love him for years. I clean her house too. Remember?"

The neighbor? The one he went to school with? The accountant? Stig told me she'd bragged about sleeping with Wilt Chamberlain! Wilt Chamberlain, the man who bragged about having more than ten thousand sexual partners, had slept with someone who may or may not have slept with my husband who slept with me? That meant that my own personal number of sexual partners could have just escalated from under ten to over ten thousand!

ACH!

"Oh sure," I answered Janina. Calmly. "The accountant. They went to school together."

"Yes, the neighbor I thought he having the affair with. She love him for years. Everybody know. Is that who he with now?" Janina asked.

"No." I answered. *Stay calm. Get tested for HIV. That mother-fucker!* "Someone else." Probably someone with another ten thousand sexual partners, most likely. Oy. The mathematician in me tried to kick in, but gave up. Is it additive? Geometric? If I'd effectively had 10,000, or 20,000, or 100,000, or a million sexual partners, why hadn't I enjoyed it more? Because it seemed just like the same old boring guy every night, who smelled like onions, snored, and farted in bed.

I should have figured it out and left him years before. Had I suspected all along? Perhaps I had, a little, now and then. But when a cheating spouse does not want to be found out, it can be difficult to find them out. I hadn't really tried. I'd trusted him. I thought he worked a lot. Because he said he did. I knew I worked a lot. I had a demanding job and two kids and two houses and two elderly parents nearby with complex medical issues. I would not let myself off the hook easily. In retrospect, though, I studied my situation carefully, even microscopically, and wondered how he had duped me for so long.

Stig had been a very busy guy. But I guess I had been busier.

I felt overwhelmed. Ruthie was depressed; Bea kept her distance. She called from college to tell me she'd pierced her nose. Perfect. Remember, she asked, when I'd pointed out that cute girl on the London Underground with a nose piercing? Three years ago? Well, she'd thought I wouldn't mind too much. Great! I was an idiot, a clueless wife, and a terrible mother! Besides which, I had a bad case of flu in February, and I thought maybe I had developed a chronic sinus infection, because my head ached nonstop. All I really wanted to do was have sex with Brad, but he was busy traveling for work.

I wouldn't say that I wanted to use Brad for sex, because I am a nice person, and I would never consciously do something like that. But I found myself completely obsessed with having sex with him, as though this would solve some problem, and at the same time I didn't want him to spend the night. I wondered what that meant. I wanted him to come over, have sex, and go home. Not even stay for dinner. Well, maybe something light, macaroni and cheese, for example. Maybe a small salad. Not too many courses. Not too much cooking or cleaning up involved. This was not a good sign. I was not even slightly into cuddling. And he was a fairly cuddly guy. I imagined myself reading the dictionary after we had sex. Out loud. To him. Interestingly, I figured he wouldn't mind. I knew I'd whup him in a game of Scrabble. So I unconsciously convinced myself that we could, under some circumstances that I could not conceivably imagine, be right for each other, and my conscious went along with it, because it was just as horny.

In mid-March, six weeks after I'd met him, I was at Brad's apartment, in Brad's bed, practically naked, finally about to have sex. But just as it was ready to happen, my head began hurting. I had had headaches every day for months, but this was more than your average headache. Back behind my eyes, in the middle of my brain. Just where it had been hurting for the past few weeks when I exercised, when I was on the treadmill, or in a kickboxing class, or on the elliptical machine, but this time I was underneath Brad, and I was so sick of the headache that instead of telling him to stop, I said nothing, because I was finally having sex! So I closed my eyes and hoped for the best. Then—suddenly—a white-hot pain shot over the top and across the back of my head, down into my neck, making it stiff, blinding me with the intensity. I opened my eyes; everything went white—I couldn't see. I felt a rush of nausea. I could barely take a breath in. I pushed Brad off of me, then rolled onto my side and waited . . . to die. This was it—the worst headache of my life. In medicine we know what that means. It means you're really fucked, you're going to die, or worse, you won't die. You'll just wish you were dead.

"Are you okay?" Brad asked. "What's the matter?"

I held my head, closed my eyes, and whispered, "I have a headache." And I waited. The pain literally took my breath away. I waited for the lights to go out, for my limbs to stop working, for my mind to stop working, for darkness to come. I waited for something—the light, the tunnel, the smell, the aura. I didn't panic, I was calm, so incredibly calm, alone, prepared. I was not afraid. It was weird. I was alone. Though Brad lay beside me, he wasn't there; I felt utterly alone.

Brad was not a doctor. Brad was not my husband. Brad was just a guy I was having sex with to whom I was not married, with whom I was not in love. I may have convinced myself I was in love with him temporarily in order to justify the sex, but I wasn't. I knew that because I was about to die. Dying makes you face the truth. And it occurred to me that I might have just had a subarachnoid hemorrhage, or a bleed in my brain, because I was having sex with someone who was not my husband whom I did not love. Did it occur to me to call an ambulance? Nope. Did it occur to me to get to an emergency room? No. I am a doctor, above everything else I am a doctor, and it never occurred to me to get medical care. Instead, it occurred to me that God was punishing me. And I wasn't even too sure I believed in God. I wasn't raised Catholic for nothing.

After lying still for fifteen or twenty minutes, thinking about my life, and that this wasn't how I would have chosen to end it, in the bed of a stranger, the headache gradually improved, and the nausea passed, though the stiff neck remained. I wanted to go home. I wanted to be *airlifted* home. I wanted to be at home with my kids, if I was going to die. I realized I didn't have any regrets, not really, not major ones, and I was ready to go if need be, but I thought it would be hard on the girls. Hard for them to lose me just now. So Brad gave me a ride, and I didn't care if I never saw him again. Both daughters were at home, and I made small talk for a while, then went into the living room and called a friend from med school, a neurosurgeon named Thomas, who happened to also work at my hospital.

"Thomas," I said, "it's Margaret."

"Hey, Margaret. What's up?"

Thomas and his wife and Stig and I had all lived a few blocks apart, back in my suburban days. I did not tell him I had had a headache while having sex with someone to whom I was not married. "Well, it's probably nothing, but I was exercising tonight, and I got this really bad headache. Really severe. With a stiff neck. Actually my neck is still kind of stiff."

"You need to get an MRI, Margaret. Tomorrow. And an MRA. That'll show the blood vessels."

MRA stands for Magnetic Resonance Angiogram.

"Okay."

"Call me tomorrow if you have problems. Call me anyway when it's done so I can look at the films."

So I slept a little and went to work the next day. My head felt the dull throbbing that now seemed my constant companion. I spent the day on the phone (and between cases) getting the runaround from my insurance company. After working all day at the surgical center, I drove to the hospital. I called Thomas from the doctors' mailroom and told him I couldn't get the test scheduled. Five minutes later he sent me to our MRI, where they'd made an opening in the schedule, and I got onto the table.

Afterward the radiologist—Alan—came out to see me. I knew he thought I was just another neurotic physician, imagining a headache was something much worse than just a headache. We're all guilty of that. We've seen the worst so we assume we have it. His face gave nothing away.

"Do you want me to go over the results with you?"

"No," I answered, and turned away. I needed time to prepare. I wanted to hear the results from Thomas.

After the scan I got in my car and drove home.

March in Chicago can be beautiful or awful. That Friday afternoon was sunny and warm, and it seemed as though everyone wanted to get home early. I sat in bumper-to-bumper traffic, head throbbing, listening to rock and roll.

My cell phone rang.

"Margaret?" Thomas's voice competed with the Rolling Stones. *"You can't—always get—what you wa-aa-aant."*

I turned the volume down.

"Your MRI showed an aneurysm. Where are you?"

"I'm driving home." My heart rate slowed, suddenly. Everything in my chest felt heavy, and nausea crept up my neck. My face was on fire. My chest pounded with every beat. Maybe I would die right now. I could feel my blood pressure rising.

My mother always told me, her daughter the doctor, that she could feel her blood pressure rising. And I always told her she was wrong. You can't feel your blood pressure, Mom.

"Maybe this isn't a good time to talk," he said.

"It's okay. Let's not put this off."

"The aneurysm is at the bifurcation of the right internal carotid artery, where it splits into the anterior and middle cerebral arteries. Margaret, that's deep in the brain. Not a very good spot. It's about fifteen millimeters. So I guess we need to talk about what we're going to do."

I might die before I got home.

"Where are you?" Thomas asked again.

"Sitting in traffic," I said.

"Listen, there's someone who specializes in aneurysms in Chicago, a really excellent neurovascular guy. I'm going to page him. Maybe he'll see you tomorrow. I'll call you back as soon as I hear something."

"Okay." I hung up the phone. It rang again almost immediately.

"Margaret, don't take any aspirin or exercise or lift anything. No strenuous activity. Just go home and relax. I'll call you back."

I drove the rest of the way in heavy traffic, trying to digest it all. I didn't cry. I thought about what to tell the kids. I called my sister Erica and my best friend Hayley. Hayley said she'd come with me to see the surgeon the next day. Erica said she'd come over that night. What would I tell the kids? The truth? I stayed calm. I am good in a crisis. It makes me good at my job. It felt almost as though it were happening to someone else. Almost, but not quite.

When I arrived home, Bea and Ruthann sat in the kitchen, planning their evening. Bea happened to be home for spring break.

"Hi guys," I said. "I need to talk to you."

I drew a diagram of the arteries of the brain on a napkin with a Sharpie and explained that an aneurysm is a ballooning of the wall of an artery that occurs where it normally bifurcates, or splits in two. The area that balloons is weak, I told them, and prone to rupture. When that happens, it's not good. My aneurysm was deep in my brain, I explained, and large. I told them that I would have to evaluate my options, but that it was treatable. I was extremely lucky to have had it diagnosed before it ruptured.

I didn't tell them that 50 percent of people die when their aneurysms rupture without warning. They simply drop dead in middle age. Or that many don't survive the treatment without a debilitating stroke. Or they die of the treatment itself. Or end up with seizures, migraines, and visual disturbances. I didn't mention any of those things.

It turns out I didn't have to. They went on the Internet and looked it up for themselves.

I took a sleeping pill that night. Hayley wrote me a prescription for Ambien. I fell asleep while writing a check. I had a big pen mark across my checkbook.

Three days later, after consulting with Thomas, another surgeon, and various specialists, I had my aneurysm treated with platinum endovascular coils by an interventional radiologist named Josh, under general anesthesia, as opposed to having an open brain procedure, at the hospital where I work. I made the decision with Thomas's help based on the size and location of the aneurysm. As the interventional radiologist said, "It isn't a question of whether you'll have a stroke if they operate. It's a question of how big it will be." The four-hour procedure was followed by a brief stay in Intensive Care. They told me I wouldn't need any further therapy. Josh said that I was as good as new. I'd missed only one week of work. I didn't have my head cut open, no shaving of my hair. Everything was done through an incision in my groin, while I was under anesthesia, put to sleep by one of my partners. I took Olga for a walk in the park the night I came home from the hospital, the night after the coils were placed.

Stig called and told me to buck up and not pamper myself. "Don't analyze it," he said.

My aneurysm was treated and cured as quickly as it had been diagnosed. It seemed almost as if nothing had ever happened.

Only everything had happened. My entire world had changed. I just didn't realize it yet.

Chapter Seven

Six weeks later I had another headache, a headache that made me think I might die. Again. Nausea, stiff neck, not as bad as the first time, but bad enough.

Working out on an elliptical machine precipitated this headache.

I called Josh, the interventional radiologist, who said, "Come right in." I drove to the hospital and got onto the table for another MRI/MRA.

Afterward he said, "Well, it looks good, and stable, but . . . It looks as though there might be some small regrowth or enlargement of the neck of the aneurysm. We need to do another angiogram to be sure."

I heard the good and stable part. It took me a half a minute to process the rest of the sentence. It took me a full minute to realize that the first half of the statement did not mesh with the second half. Regrowth is not a good thing. I wasn't yet processing what this meant.

Josh projects straightness. Proper, well mannered, meticulous, he could have been a jet pilot, or an IRS agent. His hair is neat. His clothes are tidy. Everything about him feels crisp. He practiced dentistry before becoming a doctor. He is not someone who likes to deliver bad news, particularly to a colleague.

"Is that common?" I asked. One of the reasons I chose Josh to do my procedure was that he had done more of these than anyone else in Chicago, at that time.

"Um, not really. I haven't seen it before." We stood in a dim corridor of the MRI department, in the basement of the hospital. He leaned back against a counter and looked uncomfortable.

"I'm leaving tomorrow for Tuscany, on a bike trip," I told him. My aborted anniversary trip to the Alps had given me a credit with an active travel company. I planned to fly to Rome, then meet Hayley and her husband Daniel and the rest of the group in Florence. "Do you think it's okay to go?"

"Uh, well, sure," he answered. "Hayley will be there, right?" Hayley is an anesthesiologist also—one of my partners, in fact. "When do you get back? I'll set up another angiogram for the day after. Relax. Try and have fun. Give Roseann the details before you leave today so it's all ready to go."

Italy—as they say in the brochures—is for lovers. But Italy is not particularly for divorcing, morose doctors completely isolated by a recent near-death experience who have partially treated brain aneurysms.

I met Hayley and Daniel in Florence.

Hayley and I did our residencies at the same institution and have worked together almost nonstop since then. I don't think I know anyone who takes in more details than Hayley, remembers specifics, calls more frequently to check on me, or worries more, in general, about people she barely knows. We call each other daily to discuss the tragic and miserable patients we take care of, alternately thanking our lucky stars and wondering how we can improve patient care.

Concern for others has made her chronically thin; genetics made her tall. Hayley was born to be a doctor.

Daniel suffers silently as her husband. His self-deprecating sense of humor keeps their lives in perspective. I love them both.

Hayley and Daniel were celebrating their fifteenth anniversary on the bike trip, so I left them alone as much as possible.

I don't remember much from the trip to Tuscany; I guess I was overwhelmed by the headaches and the aneurysm, stressed by what awaited me upon my return. I've forgotten conversations, dinners, names and dates, places I visited. But from Tuscany I remember three specific events.

Our group consisted of twenty bikers. I remember almost no one in particular, except that there were a lot of women, a few serious athletes, and several couples. A man on our trip, whose name we'll make up—we will call him Arnold—told me that he dry-cleans his luggage. He wore pink socks and mules and a pink oxford shirt. A friendly man from somewhere in Texas, he mentioned the dry-cleaning in passing. I have never known anyone who admits to dry-cleaning his luggage. I took that as a sign of significant disposable income.

I remember biking along a country road with Daniel early in the trip, stopping because the view was stunning and incongruous: amber waves of grain.

"Wow," Daniel said, as he pulled up alongside me. "What a view. I think I'll take a picture."

He pulled out his camera, then pedaled on.

But I stayed put.

In Italy, here were the amber waves of grain I'd been singing about my whole life, perfectly beautiful, waving, amber, the breeze catching the light so that the grain sparkled across acres and acres. I felt sucker-punched. I had no recollection of ever seeing such grain waving at me in the United States! What made me think that there was something particularly American about amber waves of grain? These were Italian grains, Italian waves, Italian amber!

But most of my time in Italy, I obsessed about death. My own death. What it would be like. I worried what my kids would do without me, how they would manage, emotionally, spiritually, psychologically. I wondered who would support them when they were down, help them recognize their own potential, be patient with them when they'd lost patience with themselves. I worried about the logistics of their lives without me. They had gotten to the age where they needed stealth parenting, indirect guidance, which sometimes required that I bite my tongue nearly in half and put duct tape over my own mouth. But it worked, more often than not. They heard me, even when they feigned deafness. I didn't think about pain, or the physical part of dying; I thought about the lack of lasting impact that people such as myself, a person such as me, makes during life, but especially after death, when your chances for any impact are gone. I thought about the little ripple that is my life, like the amber waves, flattening out over time. Life goes on. How silly it all seems. Maybe no impact should be the goal. Isn't there a saying— take nothing but pictures, leave nothing but footprints? What about that footprint?

I talked to Paul, my old anesthesia buddy, and I talked to my dad. Both of whom were dead people. The fact that I still spoke to them meant they'd had an impact on me. Would anyone talk to me after my death? Would I hear?

Some can obsess about death and make it funny, make it universal, make it something that everyone wants to read or hear about—Woody Allen, for instance. He can take neurosis and make it cute. I was feeling neurotic and decidedly not funny. I'd lost my sense of humor. Who was I? I wasn't married, I wasn't funny. I was alone and neurotic, talking to myself about wheat in Italy and obsessing about death.

Whatever social skills I once had, I lost. I could not hold a conversation with anyone about anything. I kept coming back to the near-death part. And the fact that I was still in limbo. I was going home to have more "work" done. On my brain. There was the possibility I might have a stroke, or any one of many different outcomes, different long-term problems.

Biking around Tuscany involves serious exercise. The terrain is hilly. The downhill part is fun. The uphill part is not. I hadn't exactly trained for the trip, what with the headaches and the aneurysm and all. So while biking uphill, I thought my head might blow open, especially on the really steep slopes. And yet I felt like a pansy when people passed me by. I flew downhill, out of control, and kept seeing my life flash by as I narrowly missed cars and skidded around turns.

I obediently wore my official group helmet and the reflective triangle around my waist, which attractively highlighted my backside, plus bright clothing and gloves and biking shoes while riding my red bike. The Italian cyclists, on the other hand, sped past me without helmets, smoking cigarettes while talking on their cell phones, and would routinely wave and call out, "*Ciao Bella!*" I thought, Do these guys know something I don't know? Who are they talking to? Are they talking to their mothers? I read an article once that said most Italian men wander around the planet with their cell phones plastered to their ears talking to their mothers. And why should I wear this stupid helmet when the problem was inside my head?

Toward the end of the week, I got separated from the group after leaving Montepulciano, a postcard-perfect hilltop town where we had stopped for lunch. I thought I might die getting there—biking up to the town, that is. The road up the mountain was approximately seven miles long, though the mountain seemed seven miles high. After lunch, I took off by myself and made a wrong turn down the mountain, which I then had to reclimb in order to find the right turn back down the mountain, simply because I was obsessing about death and leaving my kids alone with their father and who would teach them to make Marcella Hazan's Tomato Sauce No. 3 and how to perfectly grill a pork tenderloin and somehow I ended up alone in a driving thunderstorm on a lonesome highway *without* a cell phone. It looked like a scene from a Tim Burton movie. I speak no Italian, except a few essential words. *Sì. Birre. Agua. Nessun agnello, per favore.* I had instructions to where we were going, but no map. I'd forgotten to bring the phone numbers of the hotel and the trip leaders.

I kept pedaling along, the rain light at first, but growing progressively heavier. I stopped to put on rain gear. The sky darkened. The clouds rolled in from the far right, getting closer, and they looked dark and ominous. A single dead tree stood by the side of the road. I tried to remember the science classes of my youth. In a thunderstorm, stand under a tree? Get away from the tree? Better to stay on the bike? What the hell is the difference if your head is going to blow open at any minute? Ahead, in the far distance, I saw a lone building, a copse of trees. I biked toward it, shivering, rain pummeling my face, rain gear soaked through and through.

As I approached, there appeared an apparition. Could it be? A neon sign? Out here in the middle of Italian nowhere? *Peroni?* My mind skipped back a generation to my formative years, to Monty Python, and I heard a voice in my head repeating (in a British accent), to the rhythm of my feet pedaling the bike, *"I'm not dead yet!"*

I'd found a bar, which was the only building for miles in any direction. I took the reflective triangle off my waist and tied it around a tree in front of the building, put the bike under the porch, and went inside. I ordered a beer and hoped somebody, someday, would show up to claim me, before my head blew open.

A couple of hours later the entire vanful of bikers ran into the bar, where I sat with my feet up, reading a book and nursing a beer. I might still be there if it weren't for that reflective triangle.

Chapter Eight

BEFORE GOING TO the hospital in March for the first aneurysm treatment, I did the usual things. I gave my sister Erica access to my will and trust documents, my bank accounts, my retirement accounts, and my passwords; I gave her a set of keys, paid the bills, gave Hayley my power of attorney for health care, and asked Daniel to be the executor of my will. I made sure my house—generally speaking—was in order.

But the second time, in early June, felt different. I had a bad feeling about this. Sometimes you just know.

I wrote letters to both of my daughters. Long letters. I told them how much I loved them, what I hoped for their futures, and my favorite memories of them growing up. I told them how honored I was to be their mom. I told them the secret to making the perfect piecrust, the reason you never skip steps in baking, tricks for various vinaigrettes, and not to forget to tell people you love that you love them. I told them to work hard for what they want and have respect for themselves, and the rest will work itself out.

• • •

"I want you to do me a favor," I said to Stig. I'd called him the night before I went into the hospital.

"What kind of favor?"

"I just want you to promise me that you will give the girls my share of the Michigan house if I don't make it through this procedure."

"Why would I do that?" he asked. "It's my house."

So I was put under general anesthesia in an area of the hospital called Special Procedures, and Josh added more platinum coils. When I woke up, vomiting, in Intensive Care, I could not move my left arm.

Thomas—my old friend the neurosurgeon—stood over my bed, thin, tan, and handsome, looking very anxious. He repeatedly asked me to squeeze his hand. I couldn't. It rested limply by my side. He seemed worried, but I wasn't. I wanted to reassure him. It just felt as if my whole arm were asleep. I was completely unconcerned about this—no big deal. That lack of concern is typical of a parietal lobe infarct.

Slowly, gradually, over the next forty-eight hours, the function in my arm improved. Now only a very detailed neurological exam can detect any evidence of the stroke, or when I lift weights. I was anticoagulated, since the stroke was embolic, caused by a bit of clot sticking to a loop of coil and flicking up into my brain. I stayed in Intensive Care for three days while other little things went wrong. I had an allergic reaction to latex. I'd suspected this allergy for years, but I'd never been tested, just wore vinyl gloves at work and avoided contact with rubber. I forgot to mention it when I came into the hospital. During the night a nurse's aide gave me a sponge bath, wearing latex gloves. I developed hives from head to toe. But at least my arm started working again.

Bea and Ruthann came to visit with my sisters Bonnie and Erica. They looked terrified at all times.

Because of the stroke, and an inherited bleeding disorder called Von Willebrand disease, and the anticoagulation, and my being a physician, and it being my second go-around, there seemed a very high level of paranoia around my care. I sensed it. I felt like a celebrity who'd been caught doing something particularly unphotogenic.

This time, when I went home, I had strict orders not to work or exercise for two months. I took anticoagulants that gave me conjunctival hemorrhages, so that the whites of my eyes were red. I looked possessed by the devil. It occurred to me that I might have been so. And I had nearly constant migraines that made my vision wonky.

The day after I left the hospital, I received a phone call that I'd had an abnormal mammogram a few weeks before and needed to come back for an ultrasound-guided breast biopsy. Which of course they couldn't do because I was taking blood thinners. I started to hyperventilate. This occurred while I was driving past Crate and Barrel.

I pulled a U-turn on North Avenue and drove into the C and B parking lot. I went inside the furniture store.

And I bought a sofa. Just like that. On impulse. We didn't need a new sofa, we had a perfectly good one, but I ordered a custom-made dark red sofa, without ever sitting on the model. It did not match anything I owned, in style or color, not one other single item of furniture.

A few days later I took Olga for a walk in the park, along the side of the Diversey Driving Range. And as we walked, an errant golf ball flew over the forty-foot fence and whizzed past my head—so close, I could feel the wind against the hairs on my cheek. I stopped walking, looked up at the sky, and shouted—at God or the sky or whomever—"Enough already! I get it! It's not my time!"

I was invincible. Untouchable.

I'd survived the aneurysm, twice. The stroke. And now this golf ball that should have killed me by all rights and didn't.

I had to laugh. In one of my many fantasies, Stig died of a brain hemorrhage from an errant drive off the first tee. I'd certainly felt like a "golf widow" during my marriage. And on the day he filed for divorce, he bragged to a friend of mine, he scored the best round of his life. Way to go, Stig.

Regardless, the evidence was conclusive. I was not going to die anytime soon.

There's a certain freedom that accompanies this conclusion. Not the good kind of freedom, but the kind that makes an already crazy person seriously nuts.

I could do whatever I wanted. Nothing would touch me. I didn't know how or why, but it wouldn't. I stopped looking both ways when I crossed streets. I lost all restraint; there would be no consequences.

I know what you're thinking—I was a mom, I should be responsible, think of my kids. But I grew more and more isolated. I had a therapist, and she helped me hold on, but even so, I knew no one who had been through anything similar. I wouldn't have known what to say if I did. I was shell-shocked. I didn't even know how to begin to describe it.

On good days, I drove to my mom's house and worked in her garden. I pulled weeds, bought plants at K-mart, and put them in the ground. Olga came along, hung out in the yard, gave herself over to my mom for prolonged petting and brushing. On bad days, I stayed in the condo with migraines and watched *Seinfeld* reruns.

The practical stuff haunted me. Would my aneurysm stop growing? Josh said they couldn't add more coils. And now it was a tricky thing, even trickier than before, with all that metal in there, if they had to operate. So, stroke for sure. The third time likely would have to be something experimental. He told me about a group in Texas that was doing things with liquid Teflon . . . there were shunts . . . but my insurance would probably only pay for the procedure most likely to turn me into a vegetable. *Catch-22*.

Naturally, I did more shopping. I bought new clothes, because I'd lost so much weight that none of my old clothes fit. I bought dressy things I had nowhere to wear. Things for women half my age. When my new sofa arrived, six weeks later, I had to get rid of my old sofa. I gave it to charity. And my anxiety exploded. I had gotten rid of a sofa that matched, for a sofa that I had never sat on and did not match anything.

Bea was home from school when it arrived. She is sophisticated and petite and contained, with short red hair.

She sat down on the edge. Patted it.

She lay down on her side, her neck at a weird, acute angle. Then turned onto her back.

Then she stood, crossed her arms, and shook her head. "This is the most uncomfortable sofa I've ever sat on. It has rocks inside it. Is that what they usually put inside sofas? What were you thinking, Mom?"

"I don't know," I said. My eyes started to well up. "Do you think pillows will help?"

"I don't think a hundred pillows will help. We'll call it the Aneurysm Couch."

Brad stopped by one day and said, "I was telling my friend about having sex with you when you got that headache that turned out to be your brain aneurysm."

Shocked, I looked at him. "Really?"

"He said, 'So you basically fucked her brains out, right?'"

Brad laughed.

I didn't know what to say. Not much makes me speechless.

Life doesn't stop when you get a divorce, to give you time to adjust. Nor does it stop when you have a brain aneurysm, let you get used to it, regroup, while your divorce percolates along. Your parents get sick, the stock market tanks. Your friends may need your help when you don't feel like you have any to give. It can all happen at once. Midlife is one big snowballing cluster fuck.

I wish I could tell you what I remembered from the next year. But I can't. Not a lot, anyway.

I spent a few days at summer camp at the end of June, with my nurse friends Barb and Jan. Special Camp is run for two one-week sessions every year, and the campers are mentally disabled, some severely so. The first week's campers are eighteen and under, the second week's campers may be as old as sixty-five. Everyone who participates does so voluntarily, and this incredible effort is organized by an incredible family outside Chicago who work year round to raise money, recruit volunteers, and make it a great experience for everyone. I showed up for six years as camp doctor for the adult week. Barb and Jan, as nurses and parents of campers, taught me everything I know that has any practical application about anything—insect bites, heat stroke, sprained ankles, TLC, scrapes, asthma attacks, simple need for attention, and the like.

But it was a hard year for all three of us. "Nurse" Barb had had a stroke in April and recovered a lot but not everything. "Nurse" Jan was diagnosed with breast cancer. I'd had the aneurysm.

We slept together in a room with double bunk beds.

One night, after we'd handed out nighttime meds, Barb walked grinning into our steaming hot room where the ceiling fan twirled ineffectually. She carried a bottle of vodka and some orange juice—this illegal booty made us feel like we were underage and naughty. We'd planned and giggled and been furtive, just to celebrate the fact that we were still alive and able to toast and have a drink together. But Barb looked tired and older than fifty-eight. She seemed winded and forgetful. She went everywhere in the golf cart, whereas she used to walk.

"I have a story for you," she said.

She'd been giving out meds in the men's dorm, she explained. A dorm dad who'd had extensive military experience had gathered up the forty-plus campers in a line of sorts, to be given their medications. Most of our campers had Down syndrome, and many also had seizure disorders, hypertension, and hypothyroidism, so dispersing the nighttime meds could take a while. Because of the facial and age similarities of some of the campers with Down's, it could get confusing.

Barb stood in the middle of the men's dorm and called out name after name, getting increasingly confused by the milling about, the unrelated questions, the showing of the day's craft projects, the tales of the day's fishing expedition.

The dorm dad remarked, "It's like herding cats."

Then John, a camper who'd attended yearly since Special Camp began, noted Barb's confusion, walked up to her, and asked, "Nurse Barb? Are you retarded too?"

• • •

Her stroke turned out to be embolic, from a heart that had been invaded by amyloidosis. Barb dropped dead in August. She died while undergoing an evaluation for a heart transplant at Mayo. Not that she would have gone through with it, but what people say and what they end up doing are often two different things.

At the memorial service, I sat with Jan and another friend in front of the lawn ornament that held Barb's remains. Her best friend had bought a cobalt blue gazing ball in which to place the ashes, in her yard. So the three of us were together on a sofa at the funeral home in one of Chicago's southwest suburbs in front of a head-sized garden gazing ball telling stories about Barb. The ball looked a little like her head. It felt weird. As though she were in there, gazing back at us. I liked to think she might be.

But why was she inside the gazing ball when I was outside? Gazing in? I didn't get it. And what was worse, I didn't know how to get it. Was it all just a crapshoot?

I returned to work in August, four days a week, then quickly went to five. I also had daily migraines and began having panic attacks. This was new for me. Suddenly afraid of the most basic of anesthesia cases, I thought surely I would kill somebody. I wasn't afraid of dying myself, but the closeness I'd come to my own end felt contagious. It could rub off on the patients. I just didn't want to hurt anybody. Everything about me seemed dangerous, evanescent. Like if I touched someone, they might die instead. And the stress made me feel as if I'd forgotten everything I'd ever known.

I felt spooked. And cried constantly. Hayley called me on the phone each morning at six-fifteen while we drove to work. She would give me pep talks. She reviewed the fundamental principles of anesthesia with me, which I knew, of course. We'd talk about the cases I was scheduled to do. What I had to think about. How to handle things. On really bad days she arranged for me to do the simplest of cases.

"You're going to be fine, Margaret. You can do this."

"I know, I know," I'd say. Then my eyes would well up again.

I know I must have done other things besides anesthesia—had dinners with friends, phone conversations with friends, spent a lot of time with my mom, helped Ruthann with her college applications—but I recall almost none of it.

Is that normal after a near-death experience?

I had a lot of medical problems. I remember the migraines, going to doctors. I had a stress test. I went to see a neurology specialist for a second opinion because my own doctors were also my friends, and I needed to see someone who didn't know me, who couldn't relate to me, who had some distance. The specialist spent hours doing an exam, then proceeded to scare the shit out of me, told me if I ever had a bad headache again to get to an emergency room ASAP, because it would be serious. I ignored his advice. Seriously, life ends, you know? I just didn't want to take anybody out with me. And I wanted the headaches to go away.

The most interesting thing about that year was not about me. The experience turned me into a mirror, and so I did a lot of observing. Isolation promotes that.

I learned about my friends and acquaintances, and how they felt about their own mortality, by their responses to my brush with death.

One of my physicians asked me, "How do you get up in the morning? How do you go to work each day?" He put himself in my shoes and wondered how he would handle it.

I mentioned to an old neighbor that I'd become uninsurable—I could no longer get life, health, or disability insurance. She said, a little frantically, "So what? It's not that big a deal. I think you're overreacting."

Whereas I thought it was the insurance industry that had overreacted.

Once again—not about me—I became a recipient of her projections. She could not imagine something like this happening to her. So she could not confront what it had been like for me.

Friends declared themselves, loud and clear. And whenever that happens, it's surprising, interesting, sad, sometimes disappointing. But I never took it to be a comment on their feelings for me per se. Married people whose marriages are solid tend to stick with you when you go through a divorce. Married friends who don't want to deal with the problems in their own marriages often stay away. Friends who are terrified by the concept of their own mortality aren't comfortable when you face yours. Friends who have had to face this issue before, or who have been sick, or have thought about it with loved ones, are less fearful and less likely to abandon you. And all these thoughts occur slowly, in increments, over time.

Between the two experiences, the separation and the aneurysm, so close together, I was down a few friends.

Gradually, after about six or nine months, I started looking both ways again when I crossed the street. The haze began to clear, and I realized that I was alive, screwed up but alive, and Bea and Ruthann were depending on me. That was real. They needed me, and I needed to attend to them, and to my own version of life. And gradually, incrementally, I started living again.

Chapter Nine

IN THE SUMMER of 2004, two years into my divorce proceedings, with no end in sight and legal fees mounting, one year post aneurysm, I met a British businessman named Nigel through a neighbor, who described Nigel as "good-looking" and intelligent. For future reference, consider "good-looking" a subjective adjective. Get a picture.

I like to think I still had some brain swelling at this time, which would explain what follows. From a medical standpoint, brain swelling seems pretty unlikely, but it's possible. Anything is possible. A little swelling can account for some very bad judgment on my part.

Nigel and I had nothing in common, other than living in Chicago. His main attributes (as I saw them) consisted in having real teeth, claiming full-time employment, and owning his own home.

I admit to being a sucker for any and all accents. His British elocution immediately captivated me. And Nigel claimed to be a prolific reader (he reads! I read!), currently studying Nabokov. So when I quoted, "Lolita, light of my life, fire of my loins. My sin, my soul . . . the tip of the tongue taking a trip of three steps down the palate to tap, at three, on the teeth. Lo. Lee. Ta . . . ," Nigel was instantly entranced. And I was entranced with the thought I'd entranced him. Then he invited my daughters and me to a Cubs game. Of course, the simultaneous interest in Nabokov and my daughters completely escaped me.

But a Cubs game!

I thought this relationship had real potential.

You see, I love the Cubs. I have fond memories from childhood of watching Cubs games alone on television in the family room. Memorizing the stats. When I was in grade school and junior high, I knew the starting lineup and the batting averages of all the Cubs players. Back in those days, we had Ernie Banks and Ron Santo.

I remember Dad making fun of me, and Mom saying things like, "They're a good team, but maybe next year, honey."

"They're a bunch of losers," Dad would say.

Now, on warm summer nights, Olga and I often walk along the lakefront and look back to see the soft glow of Wrigley Field, hear the roar of the crowd when the team rarely scores. More often we hear the moan of a near miss, or watch the dejected crowd walk home.

My mother is still a Cubs fan, at ninety-one, despite or perhaps because of her dementia.

Some people fantasize about winning the lottery. Not me. I imagine leading the stadium in "Take Me Out to the Ball Game" at Wrigley Field during the seventh-inning stretch.

Anyway, Nigel and I spoke on the phone, that first week, at length.

"Tell me about being a doctor," Nigel said to me, practically purring. "What do you think about when you put a stethoscope on a person's chest?"

I know, I know, he seemed like kind of a douche bag, but I decided to withhold judgment.

He asked me out on a date, but for a week later. That seemed weird to me, to put it off that way. But whatever. Then he started calling every day, and I was a sucker for his attention. Here was an intelligent, educated man, with an accent and full-time employment, paying attention to me! And he hadn't even seen me yet! He liked my brain, even swollen. He liked my phone personality!

We ended up having a drink and dinner the day before our official date was scheduled. I could not stand the possibility that I might not find him attractive—and after all that time, daily phone conversations that lasted an hour, sometimes two hours, and because I actually hate talking on the phone, I didn't want to waste any more energy if the chemistry wasn't there.

So we met.

I can only say, in retrospect, that he did not give me the opportunity to find him attractive or unattractive. He just barreled through, taking as a given that our attraction would be mutual. And because I am used to being barreled through and over in relationships with men, the technique worked.

I told myself to keep an open mind. A real relationship develops over time, doesn't it? Looks don't really matter—what matters is the person inside. Attraction comes from knowing the essence of someone, not from something as superficial as a handsome face, a glorious physique.

So Nigel, as it turned out, was not conventionally attractive, but neither was he ugly. Nor was he pear-shaped, pockmarked, short, fat, or big-butted. However, his body habitus seemed excessively loose, jangly, with an unusually low center of gravity, like a golfer who putts extremely well. He moved with a slouchy, loping British gait that I interpreted as extreme security, a type of comfort in his own skin that seemed somewhat privileged, though ill considered. He wore good clothes, but with bright-red gym shoes, as if he were someone who could simply throw convention to the wind. Terrific! But I could not discern whether this was a fashion statement or a really bad idea. Plus, he had a way of looking at me as if he knew everything there was to know, things even I didn't know. He struck me—right off the bat—as incredibly pompous.

But as an anesthesiologist who works with surgeons all day long, pompous is just another day at the office.

"I had such an interesting day today, with a client who is having legal problems overseas," he said as we walked toward Broadway. "I almost called you to tell you about it."

"I'm not really much of a phone person," I said. "And I can't talk in the operating room." While this is not technically true, it is true when I want it to be. I can take brief phone calls at certain times. Other times I can't. But as an excuse, it's a pip.

"That's a shame," he said. "I like to call several times a day." Then he winked and grabbed my hand.

Anyway, it was easy being with him. Not, I think, because he was easy to be with, but because I am. Or rather, because I accommodate. So we had a drink, then ate sushi in my neighborhood. And planned to have our "real" date the next day.

Which we did. I was more nervous the second time we met.

We rendezvoused at a lovely Italian restaurant. He wore a suit with orange Converse high-tops, and we sat down at a nice table. Immediately he asked if I liked poetry, and before I could say no, he pulled out what he called his "favorite" book of poems. It was titled, *The Poetry of Richard Milhous Nixon*. It contained, in poetry form, excerpts from the Watergate tapes. I was relieved, to say the least. I thought, he has a sense of humor—this might work out.

It was the last funny thing he said or did for two months.

At the end of the second first date, we went to my apartment, where he met my daughters. I tried to ignore their eye rolling and the under-their-breath oh-my-Gods.

"Nigel, this is my daughter Bea—and my daughter Ruthann."

"It's nice to meet you," the girls said in unison.

"Thanks," Nigel said.

I frowned. *Thanks?*

I gathered up Olga for her evening walk, planning to accompany Nigel to his car. Near the park, before getting into his car, he kissed me, saying afterward, "I wanted to do that all night."

What an enchanting idea, I thought. He'd wanted to kiss me all night. But my mind wandered back to the moments of the night and examined each of them for kissing potential. Was it when he quoted H. R. Haldeman? Or when he told me about his various clients who risked running afoul of Sarbanes-Oxley laws? Was it when he'd talked about his father's recent gallbladder operation, or his own experiences with anesthesia and ear tubes during adolescence, with prolonged postoperative nausea and vomiting? I remembered thinking that for a man of fifty, he'd led an incredibly sheltered existence. He was pretty boring.

It wasn't that he was boring, I told myself. He was just . . . pedantic. So what if he said, repetitively, "The facts are . . . ," "At the end of the day . . . ," and "When all is said and done . . . ," and then gazed off into space to formulate his next opinion. Do they teach a course on sophistry at business school? Or perhaps just the language and appearance of sophistry?

Gradually the late-night phone calls started to annoy me. Sometimes I accidentally hung up, or nodded off, drooling into the hand piece. Mostly he talked about me, enumerating all the things he liked about me, telling me how terrific I was. Initially I found that easy to listen to. It was balm for my ravaged ego. Granted, he didn't really know me. So that felt a little wrong, a little off, like eating too many Twizzlers or Starbursts. It felt good, but I knew it wasn't good for me. I just knew I should brush my teeth after talking to him, which of course I did, since I was going to bed anyway.

And then, one evening on the phone, after a month or so, he started his nightly routine about the wonders of Margaret.

"Eh," I said, my teeth starting to ache. "Please don't do that."

"What?" I heard the confusion in his voice. He did not understand.

For a moment, I said nothing, as I tried to pinpoint my feelings—the ickyness, the unhealthiness of his attention—and I slowly recognized what I wanted to say but couldn't quite bring myself to utter the words. I could not tell him "I can't stand the constant sucking up." I couldn't say it. It wasn't polite. Mom raised me to be polite. Mom raised me to be a doormat, actually. So I said, "I'm just a little bitchy tonight—sorry. I'm exhausted. I have to go to sleep. We'll talk tomorrow."

I lay in bed that night, trying to figure out what it was about Nigel that made me want to visit a periodontist or buy a Waterpik. Suddenly I remembered that movie with Al Pacino as the devil—*The Devil's Advocate*. He finally got to Keanu Reeves through his vanity. That was it! Nigel appealed to my vanity! I didn't know I had any vanity, but Nigel had found it and exploited it.

The next morning he sent flowers, which he did every week. This had annoyed me after a week or two—enough with the flowers already. My house smelled like a funeral parlor. The card read, "Darling, Don't ever use the B word again. You're wonderful! Love, Nigel." *Don't use the B-word?* How about *bossy?* Ick. I tossed the bouquet in the garbage and sent him an e-mail.

"Nigel, do not ever send me flowers again. I mean it. Margaret."

I wanted to like him. I wanted to be in a relationship. I tried to be objective. There wasn't anything wrong with him that I could articulate. Exactly. He tried too hard.

So I decided to have sex with him, because maybe he would redeem himself. And because I was not thinking clearly. I had brain swelling, possibly. Luckily, sex turned out to be the clincher.

As a simple rhetorical question, Is there anything worse than bad sex? Men, in general, do not understand this concept, though I have heard some funny stories involving wristwatches and Chihuahuas.

But women know what I'm talking about. Women understand that not much is worse than bad sex. A really bad haircut, maybe, or an eyebrow dye job gone hideously awry can be worse than truly bad sex. But you won't laugh as much.

I suggest to you that bad sex is of value particularly when you are straddling the issue—metaphorically speaking—with regard to the relationship. Bad sex in a good relationship may cause you to rethink the merits of the relationship, and perhaps to try harder, invest in the adult entertainment industry, do whatever it takes. Bad sex in a bad relationship confirms what we already knew and should have heeded. But bad sex in a questionable relationship has the benefit of weighting the scales decisively.

Take, for example, sex with Nigel.

Things seemed promising at first. While I wasn't wildly attracted to him, I was wildly desperate and desperately bored. You would think I might have learned my lesson from almost having my brains blown out by sex with the wrong guy or the psychic trauma of the green-teddy-obsessed Ph.D. with E.D. I didn't. And who was I to talk? I may have had technically over a million sex partners by virtue of Stig, but I certainly hadn't learned anything along the way!

Anyway, Nigel liked long slow kisses with his entire tongue firmly lodged in my mouth. I prefer something more aerobic. Especially during allergy season, when ragweed and pollen engorge the mucous membranes of the nasal passages, I become a mouth breather. Who doesn't? So his technique precluded breathing on my part, forcing me to gasp intermittently for air. Perhaps he should limit himself to deep divers, I thought, or trumpet players—women with enormous lung capacity at sea level. He should not attempt foreplay at high altitude—he could kill somebody.

Immediately after removing his shirt, I got the distinct impression that Nigel had not bathed. This turns some women on. I am not one of them.

Nigel began to sweat almost immediately, and profusely. Like, maybe he had a disease or something. As my mother used to say, could it be glandular? Now, as a menopausal woman, I am sensitive to the perspiration issue. But I try to be discreet. Anyway, it wasn't particularly hot in the house—in fact, the air-conditioning was running full blast, and a fan spun furiously overhead. I might have been able to see my breath. But perspiration quickly saturated Nigel. As he worked—think heavy construction job, not sex—the sweat dripped from him, above, onto me, below. Copiously. The sweat came in large plops—*splat!*—into my eyes, causing a startled blink of self-protection.

I shut my eyes tight. It's bad enough when your own sweat drips into your eyes. But when someone else's sweat drops from above into your eyes below, that's one shared secretory event too many. And the *deed* was performed not with alacrity but with a mercilessly frenzied pace that lasted forever. I gave up trying to encourage a finale and simply tried to maintain oxygenation. Eyes closed, my imagination ran wild—I pictured myself in a yellow slicker, rain hat and Wellingtons, umbrella overhead, caught in a downpour of sexually generated secretions. I could not help it—I laughed. Yes, I did. I laughed. Between the effluent and the effluvium, this was one unfortunate dude.

We all have our defining moments. Me included.

Afterward I fled to the shower. Perhaps I waited an obligatory ten seconds, then jumped out of bed, slammed the bathroom door, and turned on the faucet. Why hadn't I installed an eyewash station at the bedside for these types of emergencies?

When I could avoid it no longer, I returned to the bedroom. Nigel wanted to cuddle. I wanted to kill myself.

Mental note: Add cyanide to eyewash station.

After Nigel, I decided to try Match.com again. Makes sense, right?

There were so many issues I did not want to deal with. I did not want to think about how I'd been carelessly dodging bullets, embracing life with recklessness, but for some reason was still alive. No, I wanted to skip that. I did not want to face the fact that Ruthann would leave for college in a couple of months, leaving me to live alone for the first time in my entire life. Let's skip that too. I especially did not want to consider why I'd stayed married for twenty years to a man I did not like, thinking that if I somehow made everything on the outside perfect, it would all turn around. And now here I was, dating men I found unappealing, hoping they would like me. Once again thinking that the right relationship could fix my life. It never occurred to me to ask myself, What do I want? What do I need? How do I fix *this*?

I simply reposted my profile and went back to dating. This time, though, I had strategy. Friends and coworkers told me horror stories about people they met online, told me how careful I should be. So I would pay very close attention to my gut instincts. I gave myself lectures. I had been an idiot with regard to dating. I would be smart! I would be circumspect! I would never give out my last name, never give out my home phone number, nor my address. I would look at the profile, try to discern obvious psychopathology, then meet for coffee. Plus I didn't feel quite so desperate. Which, of course, meant that I was more desperate than ever.

"I'm in insurance," Ron said. "An executive."

We met at an outdoor café on a warm summer evening, and he sat with his back to the corner. Ron and I definitely had different styles. He wore a white linen shirt open to midchest and a thick gold necklace. His pinky held a diamond bigger than my upper central incisor. Had I been adorned in a push-up bra and four-inch heels, we might have worked together better. Alas, I came from the surgical center, no makeup, in khaki slacks and a black blouse.

Born and raised in Jersey, Ron had lovely manners. His friends all had nicknames that began with *The*, as in Joey "The Nose" Bonanno, and Benny "The Fink" Scarmuzzo.

He looked me up and down and said, "So you're really a doctor?"

I smiled. "Why do you find that hard to believe?"

"I don't know. When I think of doctors, I don't think of dames like you."

"What's your mental image of a doctor?" I asked Ron from Jersey.

"Eh . . . Marcus Welby, I suppose. Some old guy with white hair wearing a glove who's gonna stick a finger up my ass." And then he winked.

I burst out laughing.

Alcohol was invented for precisely these situations. Two glasses of wine to one of Ron's martinis, and we totally enjoyed each other's company. We stayed for dinner. I laughed as he told me about cheating on his wife with a twenty-five-year old, whom he'd then grown tired of.

"She wasn't smart enough," he confided.

I nodded sympathetically. "That can happen."

"That husband of yours, you want him offed?" Ron asked. "He could meet with an accident. Nobody'd be the wiser. I know people."

"Oh, that's so nice of you," I said. Were all people from Jersey this generous? "Do you have a card?"

We shook hands at the end of the night, and Ron kissed my cheek.

"You want to see me again, you call me," he said.

Not my type, but a real gentleman.

Next I met Larry, a real estate investor from Wicker Park.

His picture on Match portrayed a boyishly handsome, brown-haired fifty-year-old. We spoke on the phone—his life seemed complicated by young children and a job that involved extensive travel. The travel didn't bother me, though he spent an inordinate amount of time discussing airline mileage programs. We agreed to meet on a weeknight for dinner at an upscale restaurant of Larry's choosing between our two neighborhoods.

Larry stood when I arrived at the table. Maybe six feet tall, he wore a blue work shirt, chinos, and a tweed jacket.

We shook hands and sat.

"The owners are friends of my ex-wife's and mine," Larry said, by way of opening the conversation.

"Oh," I said, and looked around the restaurant. I saw a neighbor of mine with a young woman who I knew was not his wife. I waved.

"Do you like halibut?" Larry asked. "The halibut is great here."

"Not really," I answered. To me, halibut is like an empty chalkboard. I glanced at the menu. I remembered why I never ate at this restaurant. I'm a picky eater, and they had a tendency to pair things I hated—like Brussels sprouts, fennel, spinach, polenta, lentils, and beets—with just about anything I did like. Usually there were two or more things I disliked paired together with something I liked. I never knew what the proportions would turn out to be, so I had a hard time finding anything to order.

The waitress came to the table. "Would you like to order a cocktail?"

Larry answered, "Nothing for me. I'll just have water." Then he looked at me and said, "I have to work tonight."

Perfect.

"I don't," I said, and turned to the waitress. "I'll have a glass of wine. Something white, please."

"We have a Pinot Grigio, a Chardonnay, and a Sauvignon Blanc."

"I'll have the Chardonnay," I answered, and looked at Larry.

He smiled.

Time stood still for Larry's defining moment—the moment of his smile.

As a physician, I feel I should be prepared for every aberration, every ailment, each and every physical anomaly that life throws my way. I should be above a pure gut response, and I should have the ability to handle humanity's variances with equanimity and aplomb without betraying any obvious emotion. And I probably did, in retrospect, or most likely I handled it relatively well. My mouth didn't drop open; I don't think I frowned, gaped, or gagged; I surely didn't hurl or show any obvious sign of my horror. But when Larry smiled, he revealed such deep dark brown teeth as to make the rest of him seem incongruously alive. Were they covered in shoe leather? Diseased in some tropical, fungal, putrefying way? I was instantly mesmerized. I simply could not look elsewhere. They were riveting. They were hypnotic. I wanted to know the natural history of this disease, whatever it was, but couldn't think of a way to work the question into our conversation. My mind rummaged through remote lessons on dental pathology, searching for possible causes of Larry's malady. The rest of the evening passed in a blur— all I remember was Larry's teeth, and thinking, Whiteners! Thirty dollars! Costco!

"How did you get here?" Calvin asked. It brought to mind the Talking Heads lyric, *How did I get here?*

But that wasn't what he meant.

Calvin wore makeup. I kid you not. Foundation, a touch of mascara. It made me wonder, is that common among men? Calvin, a retired trader, met me at a Near North outdoor café on a Sunday morning for brunch. He was not bad looking, in a long-haired poodle sort of way. But the makeup struck me as . . . singularly odd. Had dating strategies changed in twenty-five years? Were men wearing makeup now? I tried to keep an open mind.

"I took the bus." I answered. As opposed to a space ship or truly alternative modes of transportation.

"Really? I don't think I've ever been on a bus," Calvin said, looking thoughtful. "Maybe in Europe."

Calvin proceeded to tell me, in the first ten or fifteen minutes after we sat down, before we even ordered omelets, about his ex-girlfriend who had filed assault charges against him, though to hear him tell it he had done absolutely nothing wrong whatsoever, nope not even the slightest thing to account for being put in hand-cuffs in front of his children and hauled off to jail for the night. "I hardly touched her!" he said. Then he went off on a rant against police officers in general, commenting on the low intelligence required by the field, though he may have used the word *stupid*, and how everybody overreacts to the word *felony*.

"So," Calvin asked conversationally, "where do you live?"

I waved my arms in large, vague circles indicating south and shook my head simultaneously. "North."

"But where?" Calvin wanted details. I wracked my brain to remember if I'd talked to him from my home phone or my cell. Could he trace anything?

"Way north," I said. "Really, really far . . . north." North of the north pole. Farther than that.

Gita, my former therapist, says that most people tell you exactly who they are in the first five minutes of meeting them.

Jeremy, an oboe player for a local symphony, did exactly that.

"Hi, Margaret. It's na-na-na-na-nice to mm-mm-mm-mm-meet you. Would you like a drink?"

I shook his hand and sat down. "Yes, please." Ten. Maybe more.

In a heartbeat, I found myself back in the little room at the top of the stairs of the second floor of my grade school, the speech therapy room, where a nice young woman whose name I've forgotten treated me for years for a lisp that still comes out when I'm really, really tired.

But it wasn't the stutter that I found problematic. It was Jeremy's wandering eye. One eye looked at me; the other eye looked at my left ear. I think.

Here I'd finally found a man of metaphor, but given my marriage, with the cheating husband and all, it was the wrong metaphor! A wandering eye—no thank you.

"So you're a doctor," Jeremy said.

"Yes, an anesthesiologist."

"I have a s-s-s-seizure disorder."

"Oh—I'm sorry," I said.

"But it's really only a problem when there's a change in air pressure, like on airplanes."

I found myself nodding. How exactly do I respond to that declarative sentence? People really do tell you who they are in the first five minutes. But the question is—why?

I guess it's because we're all lonely, and hurting, among other things. We want to find someone sympathetic, someone who will want us again. We want to be heard. And so we head out onto the trail, thinking that if we find that right person, the right "whump," say the right thing, we will make it all okay.

We are all looking for a quick fix for a bone-deep problem that there is no quick way to fix.

Here's the thing: people going through a divorce are wounded. We don't want to admit how wounded we are, even if we're glad to be out of a bad marriage; we don't want to know how much work it takes to heal, how much time it will take. But we are bleeding from every orifice. Even if we were to meet the "right" person, we would either (a) screw it up, (b) not recognize him or her, or (c) both. More likely we will meet someone who is attracted to our fractures, turned on by the sight of blood.

My own personal fractures were so complicated by then, by the marriage, by the divorce, by the aneurysm, by the bad dates and the worse sex and the aneurysmal sex, that I was bleeding for everyone to see. I attracted predators. And I didn't have a clue.

Chapter Ten

IN SEPTEMBER 2004 Ruthann left home for college.

Hayley and Daniel and Kate and Neal and my friends Andrea and Ben and all three sisters called daily, sometimes multiple times, each asking the same thing:

"Are you okay? Are you lonely? Want to have dinner?"

I'd flown with Ruthie to New York City to help her get settled. We attended orientation events, figured out where her classes would be, and learned how to get from the dorm to campus. It took a couple days of frantic shopping, organizing, and schlepping to squeeze my free-spirited daughter into a microscopic dorm room.

"You going to be okay, Mom?" she asked as we wandered through a multilevel Kmart in the East Village. We'd been through a lot together—a few trips to the hospital, a lot of tears, a three-day weekend consisting of four seasons of *Felicity*. But it was time for her to get on with her life, to have her own future. The time had come for her to stop being oppressed by my life.

"I'm going to be fine," I said. "And how about you?"

She smiled. "It's pretty cool here, doncha think?" I knew she would thrive at NYU. She had three charming roommates and several friends from high school already in New York. She seemed ready for college.

We stood on the corner of Eleventh Street and Third Avenue and hugged. I held her tight. Finally I let go, hailed a cab, and said, "LaGuardia."

When Bea left for college three years earlier, I'd done mental preparation for months ahead of time. Bea separated herself. We argued. She helped me prepare. I helped her. Ruthann couldn't wait to be an only child. But we'd been an intact family then. We supported each other. Stig was the one who'd lost it when Bea left for Kenyon, as though he hadn't had eighteen years to prepare. He had been so crazy while we were packing—at one point Bea, Ruthann, and I locked ourselves in the bathroom. We couldn't stand his screaming anymore.

"Nobody, in the history of the world, has ever taken this much stuff to college! I won't allow it!! Don't they have sheets there? Don't they have blankets, or pillows?"

We took two cars, and the kids drew straws—short one had to drive with Stig. When we got to Ohio, to the Kenyon campus, he saw some fathers with a full-size refrigerator on a dolly, pushing it into a dorm room.

He sat down on the curb, defeated, and said, "Okay. I get it now."

The next morning he cried.

But when Ruthie left, it had been just she and I living together for two years. We hung on to each other until the last possible second. I hadn't prepared. She wouldn't let me. How do you prepare for an amputation?

• • •

When I arrived back in Chicago to an empty condo, I waited for the loneliness to set in. Olga and I took long walks. I swore I would take good care of myself—I would eat healthy and actually cook meals, no peanut butter and jelly sandwiches with a Diet Coke each night while standing alone in the kitchen. I would exercise regularly and actively manage this new phase of my life. So I waited. But the loneliness didn't come. After a week, I realized, it wasn't going to. I liked living alone. I was forty-six years old, and alone for the first time in my life. I didn't have to take care of anyone except myself. And the dog. And my mom. And my patients, of course. And the kids, when they came home. But what a change! What a pleasure! I could bike, and read, and see friends, find time to do the things I'd been postponing. I'd kept my profile up on Match.com, more out of idle curiosity than anything. I'd grown disenchanted with the concept of Internet dating. Not that I knew of anything better.

And then, in late September, I received a Match e-mail from a man named Alex. He didn't have a profile posted, he said, because of the nature of his job. Over several pages he told me about himself in a way that was articulate, funny, and obviously educated. He sent a picture, which looked serious, slightly sad. He was much older than me and a recent transplant from Canada.

Olga and I drove to Michigan for the weekend. We'd put the house up for sale, and until it sold, Stig and I shared it—he took one week, I took the next. I'd invited an older couple from work to spend the weekend. On Saturday afternoon, they went for a bike ride while I took the dog for a long walk on the beach. When I returned to the house, I wrote to Alex.

I told him that I'd had some not-so-good experiences with

Match.com and preferred to meet men for a drink, not dinner. In fact, I preferred to rendezvous like police officers, in cars facing opposite directions, with engines running, perhaps share a dough-nut. Or we could meet at a drinks kiosk at the Chicago North-western train station, like characters in a John Cheever story, all suburban angst and middle-aged ennui (or the other way around, depending on the suburb). For a week we exchanged e-mails, easy, and light. I liked his sense of humor.

We met on a Wednesday evening in early October. Alex was gregarious, intelligent, and outrageously funny. I asked him about his work—he jokingly referred to himself as a man of independent wealth who worked to fill his days, but didn't elaborate. I found him attractive, despite our age difference. We talked for three and a half hours; he told me he'd lost his wife after a long illness. Still we managed to laugh. I had a wonderful time. I thought he seemed bright and compelling. I smiled the whole way home. And yet for some reason, I didn't think he'd ever call. He'd offered me a ride, but I felt awkward taking it, as though I would be putting him to too much trouble. I jumped into a cab instead. I was nervous and shy. But then I've always been shy. I'd finally found someone I liked, and I had no idea what to do about it.

I e-mailed him, saying what a wonderful time I'd had, giving him my phone number.

He sent a noncommittal response to my thank-you note. Then I sent another e-mail: "Do I have to ask you out?"

He responded, "You jumped into a cab without even a hand-shake, kiss, a hug. What am I to think?"

I e-mailed an apology, acknowledged my clumsiness, and stated I'd be happy to give him a belated kiss for the first date if and when he came to dinner.

His last e-mail, before he came to dinner, said, "Thanks for the invitation and the effort. I haven't had anyone cook a meal for me in a couple of years. I don't know if I will know how to act so tread cautiously."

He came to dinner. I did not take the advice about treading cautiously. I wish I had.

Alex had disaster written all over him. I saw it, and I ignored it. It had been six months since his wife died; for complex reasons, he had only begun to grieve. His responsibilities overwhelmed him. He sought respite from them and from his grief. He found me.

To be fair, I had disaster written all over me too, but I didn't think along those lines. I was barely a year past my aneurysm. I had not begun to process what it all meant. I desperately wanted someone to make me feel safe again.

In retrospect, I suppose Alex really just wanted to have sex, though I'm not sure, even now. I know I wanted much more than that. I wanted security. I wanted a future. I wanted someone who could make me feel that I was worth something again. I wanted someone else to provide all those things, because I was not capable of providing them for myself.

I never thought I was someone that the average guy would date simply for the purpose of having sex. I'm attractive enough, but I am not a simple person. I analyze everything. I read constantly. I do not play dumb. I'm more educated than most men I meet. As Stig told me for twenty years, "Men might find you attractive, but only until they find out how smart you are."

And you would think, wouldn't you, that I would be cautious by now? In fact, it was the opposite. I couldn't wrap my head around caution. When you don't know if you're going to live or die, what's the point of it?

Live each day as if it's your last, someone told me. Well, I actually did that.

Or I thought I did. With Alex, I put blinders on. He was the first man I'd met who'd given me hope for the future, and I fell hard for it and him. He could be wonderful, and help me with complex business problems and strategy. Or he could be awful. He played coy, withheld just enough to tantalize me, and I fell for that too. He undertipped at restaurants and in taxicabs. I ignored it. He treated me as a temporary player in his life, introducing me as his "date" after we'd been together for five months. I ignored that too. He grabbed me in public, as if he were a horny schoolboy, sliding his hand under my skirt when he thought no one was looking. It annoyed me—I slapped his hand away—but I tolerated it. When I finally became really angry he wouldn't speak to me. I suffered from a surfeit of compassion and a paucity of judgment. I didn't want to lose him, for no good reason.

Together we behaved as if there might be no tomorrow. Alex turned out to be perfect in that regard, because he too needed life-affirmation or something, out of grief, or survivor guilt, or anger, or some complex emotion I'll never understand, and I wanted to feel wanted. His startling virility may have been an aberration for him—a once-in-a-lifetime event. Or maybe that's just how he was made. I don't know. He wore me out in more ways than one.

As a physician, I've come to think of life in terms of a bell curve. Or maybe it's the mathematician in me. Either way, Alex definitely pushed the limits of the X-axis.

Anyway, after a couple of months, he said, "Tell me a story."

"What kind of a story?" I asked, frowning.

"Any kind, something sexy, something . . . unusual."

At first this was easy enough. Eager to please, with a relatively vivid imagination, I ran through the obligatory schoolteacher, nurse, librarian, tollbooth worker, high-rise window washer, and flight attendant fantasies, which I made up as I went along, catering to his Democratic taste. But after a while I risked repeating myself, and for some reason that felt wrong. Repeating the same sex fantasy would be equivalent to wearing the same gown to a hospital function twice in one year. My peers would think I didn't have anything else in my closet.

I had to diversify.

Of course, I never did any prep work. I waited until the last minute. I waited until we were in flagrante delicto. Then I frantically searched my brain for material. But the only thing I could come up with were the myriad ways in which I'd been killing off Stig in poetry, short stories, and unfinished novels for the past twenty years, none of which made very good material for sex fantasies. I'd killed him off so many times, without him actually dying, I finally had to leave him. He wasn't going to die. Not soon enough to suit my purposes. So I tried to think of an adaptation.

There was the fishing scene.

Picture yourself in a small boat on a serene lake in northern Wisconsin on a warm summer afternoon, the sun setting, nary a ripple on the water. You reach for a cool beer, draw a long, refreshing draft. Then suddenly a wasp that's been swimming in the can stings you, causing your tongue to swell up twenty times normal size, which cuts off your airway, cuts off your oxygen supply, and you suffocate. You are all alone in the great North Woods, grasping your throat, turning a hideous shade of dusky blue before falling backward over the edge of the dinghy into the water, only to wash ashore days later, a giant bloated misshapen mess.

Even worse, the elusive largemouth bass you'd pursued your entire fishing life circles your dead body and gets the last laugh.

Okay—now somehow make the fishing scene sexually appealing, even provocative. *Not so easy.*

Unless the guy is into autoerotic asphyxiation, or sex with largemouth bass (and you know there are fishermen out there with that going on), it may be difficult to adapt the fishing scenario to the bedroom.

I had other stories, but generally speaking, the guy always died—though occasionally he simply succumbed to a prolonged vegetative state. And the stories tended to be gruesome—a lot of blood, occasional dismemberment, a rare decapitation—because I was killing off my husband, not trying to seduce a lover. Sometimes I could be generous—I gave him a deadly cancer, something tragic and quick, but adequate time to say *aloha* to the loved ones.

The widow, on the other hand, typically went on to lead a full and fabulous life. She found love and happiness, despite having left a veritable graveyard behind her. She lived to ripe old age, wearing sequins: think salsa dancing, not shuffleboard.

Not so sure that was gonna turn him on.

Though we traveled together and usually had fun, his ungentlemanly public displays of affection made me uncomfortable. When I objected, he withdrew behind a wall of guilt, his grief still fresh, unprocessed.

"I feel empty," he said, more than once.

After an argument he told me, "I don't love you, and I never will."

We hadn't been talking about love.

Ruthann said, "Mom, I don't like you when he's around. You

get quiet. You aren't yourself. It's like he takes up all the space in the room and doesn't leave any for the rest of us. He just takes over. Aren't you tired of men like that?"

Bea put it more simply: "I don't like him."

My mom met him once and gave her opinion: "He's overbearing, and too old for you."

Despite the input of my loved ones, I was crazy about Alex, or maybe I was just crazy. I could not differentiate. It seemed like love, but without any warmth or willingness on his part. So much damage had occurred to the two of us, love seemed an impossible goal, a quaint anachronistic concept. And yet I remained hopeful. I saw the potential instead of the man.

After six months I asked if he would be available to have dinner for my birthday, with some friends.

"No," he said. "I'll be out of town."

"What about the week after?" I asked.

"I'll be gone then too."

Silence. I heard the sound exactly as he intended it.

Alex withdrew for his own reasons. He didn't explain.

"I can't do this," he said, and never called again.

For a few brief months with Alex, I felt almost safe. I liked the feeling, as deceptive as it may have been. Perhaps it derived from the good financial advice he gave me, or the way he helped me in practical matters; he had strength in areas where I had weakness. Maybe it was because he too knew that safety is only an illusion, that everything can change in an instant. It often does. Alex, with the loss he had suffered, knew that too well.

After Alex, especially after the way he ended things, I felt that vulnerability all over again. I felt it acutely. I was never really safe.

Certainly not in my marriage. Certainly not in my health. Not in my feelings for someone. Not really ever.

But on occasion I wonder, had we met a couple years later, when we were both healed and whole, when I could hold my own, after his grief had lessened, if we might not have had a more lasting go at it.

Then I think again and I know I dodged another bullet.

Chapter Eleven

Two thousand five turned into a defining year, meaning a year we do not want to repeat.

Annus horribilis, as Queen Liz would say.

Early in the year, in the dead of winter, when the snow lay thick on the ground, the events of the past finally caught up to me.

Olga and I took the same path most nights; she liked the routine. I wore headphones sometimes and listened to music. Sam Cooke, Van Morrison, Alanis Morissette. In the frigid cold I found myself staring at the running path lights: they would blink, turn on and off as I stood underneath, which seemed weird. It happened repeatedly. I moved down the path. The same thing happened with the next light. Really weird.

The only person I knew who had been through a near-death experience—a former NFL player—walked with me one night and also noticed the lights blinking on and off.

"Someone is messing with you, girl," he said.

"What do you mean?"

"I mean, somebody is talking to you. Through the lights."

"They're not on motion detectors?"

"Have you ever seen a motion detector work that way? Turn off when you move toward it?"

"Well, no," I said.

"Who do you think it is?" he asked.

"You mean like, a dead person?"

"Mmm-hmm."

I tried to think who it might be.

Either Paul or my dad.

This looked like Paul's work.

We'd always joked that my dad, an engineer, could not screw in a lightbulb. Plus Dad died in old age, ready.

My struggles involved a near-death experience in midlife; Paul had had his own before he succumbed. And didn't Paul love to give me advice?

We'd been introduced by Martin, another anesthesiology partner, on Paul's first day at the hospital. He'd generated some buzz even before he arrived—a divorced man! So of course I immediately wondered which of my friends he could date. Before I even met him. That summarizes the problem with fix-ups.

We became fast friends, Paul and I. In the mornings I would leave the women's locker room to find him at the soda machine, buying breakfast.

"You're lookin' scrawny, Overton," he'd say with a wink.

"You're not," I would respond. "And Pepsi is not breakfast food, Paul."

He gave me books—I gave him articles. I didn't read a lot of the Buddhist stuff he pressed on me, not at first anyway. I read the Alice Munro stories. And the Jung. But I stopped reading fiction for a long time after he died. It required a leap of faith I could no longer make.

The staff loved him—the ones who didn't have yardsticks up their butts—for his irreverence and his sense of humor. I loved him because he said out loud what a lot of us thought but didn't say. He kept our department in balance on money issues, called people on their greed, and generally provided us with a soul. He insisted on an openness that was healthy, forcing us to look at our ethics as well as our care of patients. We were a different department back then.

On Labor Day 1996, a few months after his heart attack when he was back at work, Paul and I sat side by side on a low sofa in front of the TV in the nurses' lounge while I ate a vending machine dinner. I was on trauma call.

The south window faced the doctors' parking lot. From our vantage point we could watch the planes coming in a line from the east to land at O'Hare.

"What's going on?" Paul asked, taking a Frito out of my bag.

I felt terrible—it had been a beautiful day outside, and I'd just finished a long, exhausting trauma case. A young girl had been injured in a car wreck, and it looked bad for her, though we'd gotten her out of the operating room and up to ICU, barely alive. I still had twelve more hours of call to go. I was younger then, still impatient, struggling with what it meant to do the job I was doing. I felt angry at the girl for not wearing her seatbelt, for ruining my day, for making me work so hard to save her life when I knew there was no freaking way she'd survive beyond the next day or two. I'd seen miracles, but mostly I'd seen people like her turn out to be vegetables, if they survived at all. Meaningful life seemed unlikely. And I was not as clear on my boundaries back then. "The patient is the one with the disease," as Samuel Shem put it in *The House of God*. I felt disgusted with myself—for not having more tenacity and patience and compassion. I had the skills, but I took it personally—every death felt like a failure.

"That trauma surgeon, Vasquez, is such a putz," I said.

"Yeah, we know this. What did he do to piss you off?"

"He's up to his elbows in blood in a dying kid's abdomen, and he has the nerve to complain to nurses who make a fraction what he makes about his wife's spending habits. In the operating room! Doing a trauma! I think that makes him qualify as a putz. Don't you?"

"Depends on how much she's spending . . ."

"Spoken like someone with three ex-wives."

"You want to hear my theory about doctors?" Paul asked.

"Do I have a choice?"

"No. You have someplace better to go?"

"Well, not at the moment."

"Fine. Shut up and listen, Overton."

"Feel free to opine, doctor." We smiled at each other then, a snarky sidelong glance that spoke volumes. We were buddies, partners in derision, pals in the trenches. I could count on him and vice versa. He nudged me with his elbow, but then he turned serious.

"I think that medical training demands so much time and commitment, from a young age onward, that the price you pay is in life experiences, sweetheart, and in growth. Emotional, psychological, spiritual growth. You spend all your time and energy committed to pre-med, then med school, then residency, all focused on the next goal—the goal of being a doctor, of passing the boards, of getting the right fellowship, then the right job, that we become experts in delayed gratification."

"I don't know. Immediate gratification is for drug addicts, right? Is that the alternative?"

"I'm not finished," he said.

"Sorry."

"Then you get out, you're saddled with debt, you have a few years to build a practice, you pay off the debt, but in truth, after five or ten years, you have the perfect combination of fresh training and some experience. Then you realize—you're there. This is it. You're as good as you're ever going to be. Only there's nothing left to strive for. You've never grown up enough to realize that you're not the center of the universe. You're working hard for patients, and reaping monetary rewards, but there's this little problem—you're not satisfied. You lack fulfillment. So all of a sudden, you're in your mid- to late thirties, or early forties, and you say to yourself, now what? Is this all there is? Because it feels incredibly hollow. You've got no hobbies, no true friends to speak of, no real interior life, you don't know what to do with yourself, so you begin to acquire stuff to fill the void. Cars, houses, toys, things, 'cause you can't stand being still or alone. And you haven't got a fucking clue as to why you aren't happier."

I stared at him, but he seemed mesmerized by the planes in the distant view through the window.

"Jesus. That sums up just about everybody I know."

"Maybe," he answered, and took a breath. "Look around you, Margaret, look at your doctor buddies. A lot of them are not nice people. They're jerks. Not just Vasquez, though he's typical. They're boring, demanding, difficult. They spend a lot of money on shit they don't need, either to appease their wives or their egos." He took the empty Fritos bag from my limp hand and threw it at the garbage can. It landed on the floor.

"Doctors are practically trained to be assholes," he said. I took a breath. Paul leaned down to pick up the Fritos bag, patted it flat, thoughtfully, with his fingers. "You work your butt off, and the system convinces you that if you don't work until you drop, you aren't dedicated, you aren't a real doctor, and therefore you could kill somebody. Above all, do no harm, remember?"

I nodded. That about summed me up.

"So it's midlife crisis time. Affairs, bungee jumping, marathon running, sports cars, wine collections, you name it. Remember when what's-her-name got her belly button pierced? I think it's worse for men than women, because women physicians—I don't know—at least those who have kids usually seem a little more grounded."

I just sat and stared at him. "That's my life," I whispered.

He smiled at me then. A big, kind, gentle smile. A sad smile. "No, sweetheart," he said, "it's not. It's my life. That's how I know."

He stood up, facing me, and slapped his paper OR hat against his leg. He towered over me. "Or at least it used to be. Before I grow'd up."

Paul turned and stared out the window at the nearly empty parking lot and at the sky, where the sun sank over the airport. I studied him—the profile, the straight stubby nose, the way he rubbed his hat across his bald head, then settled it in place.

I thought about the differences between men and women. I was too busy and too tired and too frazzled and too needed to ever have a midlife crisis, or so I thought. It was a luxury I'd never be able to afford, like a foot massage. But men—I guess they're raised to have higher expectations of their careers than women have, than I had. I just thought I'd earn a decent living. Help people. I didn't ever expect to be important. Maybe my midlife crisis would come later. Have different antecedents.

"Is that your life, Paul?" I asked. "You seem all grown up to me—of course you are ten years older. But I don't know—I struggle with this doctoring stuff—you seem to take it all in stride."

"That's now, Margaret. Look at what I've been through."

"It seems like you've made your peace with it," I said. "You're looking at it. That's the important thing. Right?" I closed my eyes and leaned my head back. When I opened them, I said, "What are you still doing here anyway? Isn't it time for you to go home? Take a nap?"

"Yeah. I guess I'll take off."

He leaned down then, and placed his hand on the top of my head, let his palm linger on my hair. "Hope you have a quiet night."

He was dead less than four months later.

And now he was talking to me through the lights on the running path?

This is a binary system, these lights. On, off. If you are going to send me a message, pal, it's got to be a simple one.

I replayed that day, those words, that conversation in my head so many times. The questions I should have asked—how do I ask them now? How did he grow up? Was it the heart attack? The divorces? Was it some patient he took care of? Some combination of them all?

I felt my consciousness opening up. When I interviewed patients preoperatively, I had several who told me that they'd had brain aneurysms. I felt compelled to tell them I too had had a brain aneurysm.

One woman, in her early seventies, took my hand and said, "We're the lucky ones, aren't we? I hear of so many who don't make it."

My eyes welled up. I nodded.

Another patient, a gentleman in his sixties, said, "Don't you wonder, 'Why not me?' Why does someone else drop dead, and I'm alive?"

I stared at him. I nodded. Yes, I want to tell him. I wonder that constantly. But I say nothing. I can't speak without losing composure. And today I am responsible for his well-being. I haven't yet learned how to do both.

Fifty percent of people with bleeding aneurysms present with sudden death. To have a symptom, to survive a bleed, is unusual. We are lucky. We've dodged a bullet.

My whole career I believed that we, in medicine, rarely save a life. I believed that people usually die when it's their time.

I could not put it all together. I did not sleep. I walked the dog, hour after hour, noticing odd things in the park. Birds chirped loudly. It felt as if they were speaking directly to me. Raccoons stopped their nighttime climbs at my eye level, peering around tree trunks. Olga watched them, calm. She did not flinch. We moved on. I'd begun to feel as if I were here for a reason. I wished I knew what it was.

I dodged a bullet, but there was a bullet out there with my name on it.

Where's the luck in that?

So I took a trip to Graceland, to search for enlightenment.

Could there be a better place?

"People down here, honey, we don't call it Graceland," Rae told me. "We call it Elvis's house."

My friendship with Rae stretches back to childhood. We met

when I was six and she was eight. Our dads were close friends. She's lived in Memphis since college.

Rae is tall and blonde and beautiful, runs marathons, and does hair for a living.

"We used to go out to Elvis's house, and party in his living room. Then around midnight, he'd come downstairs, all fat and puffy-eyed, make an appearance, you know? Stay five minutes, then go back upstairs."

Rae indulged my need to do the Graceland tour, have our pictures taken, and buy Elvis dancing-pelvis kitchen clocks. She waited patiently while I picked out postcards with his recipes for pecan pie and meatloaf to send all my friends in Chicago. I really wanted to buy vials of Elvis sweat, but they weren't selling any. So instead I settled for a somber baby-blue T-shirt with dark blue lettering: *Graceland.* I could be buried in this, I thought. *Return to Sender* was my second choice.

Before I left Memphis, Rae's neighbor read my tarot cards. Whatever he saw scared him so much, he could barely discuss it with me. He was young with dyed blond hair and wore yellow pants.

"Be careful, honey," he said. I had never met this man before.

In May, Bea prepared to graduate from Kenyon College in Gambier, Ohio, with a degree in psychology.

"I want nothing to do with psychology, ever again," she told me, and said she planned to move home to look for a job in anything-but-psychology.

Most of my family came to Gambier for the graduation to show their support for her accomplishment, including three sisters with one husband and one boyfriend, two nieces, a nephew, and my mom. Stig showed up with his girlfriend and her dog. I brought the fifteen pounds I'd gained since the breakup with Alex.

The commencement was held outdoors, on a perfect spring day. Kenyon's traditional stone buildings lent a distinguished air, and the quad was lined with chairs. Bea and her friends had organized events for the parents and families all weekend long, organized brunches and dinners and barbecues, so that we could finally get to know the other parents and students with whom they had lived and shared the past four years.

David Foster Wallace gave the commencement address.

It didn't seem as though many people listened. Certainly my own family barely paid attention—and no one else seemed to grasp the import of his words. I didn't blame them—the sunny day, the chirping birds, the gentle breeze distracted. He was a "kid" standing many feet away wearing academic dress at a podium where imperfect acoustics made it essential to strain your ears to hear what he had to say. And it has become the default setting to tune out these institutional sermons. But I'd stopped eating lobster, for God's sake, based on his article in *Gourmet*! Was it just the year before? He was a hero to me, as much as a hero to my kids and their friends. We were close in age, and closer than I realized in temperament. There he stood before us talking about compassion, and wasn't that the real value of education? Wasn't that the real value of life?

I leaned against a tree and cried.

This is water, he concluded. This is water.

When I returned home to Chicago, my divorce trial began. Only about 5 percent of divorces go to trial. Typically those that do go to trial involve complex child custody issues. Mine did not. My divorce went to trial because my aneurysm rendered me uninsurable, and because my employer offered no health insurance. Isn't that funny? A large group of doctors without group health insurance? Hilarious.

Stig also brought some issues to his side of the equation.

I won't go into details, but it was heartbreaking, ugly, and unnecessary. It felt as though I were visiting the heart of darkness, every day, for three weeks. I had reached the Marlon Brando part of *Apocalypse Now*.

The American system of justice, at least of the divorce court variety, is very, very broken.

I left the courtroom each day and went directly to my health club to go swimming. Complete immersion—self-baptism, as it were—seemed the only way to get the courtroom off me. I was beyond thought. Moving through water helped. Wallace's words helped. I kept a copy of the commencement address on my computer and reread it every few days.

I wore pearls to the courtroom. Pearls are the female version of a bespoke suit and a Hermès tie. Pearls around a woman's neck say to the world, *Don't fuck with me.* I know, they look so Republican, seem so proper. But they work wonders.

Pearls do not have to be real. They can be cheap, they can be cultured. They can be a forty-dollar strand, as long as they don't flake on your clothing. But when a woman puts on a strand of pearls, she is saying to the world, *I am a force to be reckoned with.*

When I was on the witness stand—the three days they kept me there—I didn't need the pearls. I was telling the truth. But they lent me a sangfroid before I ever opened my mouth, and they instilled a confidence in me I didn't know I was capable of. When I sat in the courtroom and listened to the case against me, pearls gave me strength.

Stig, in the end, would provide health insurance through his job, though we could not agree on the details. At least COBRA would last three years. I would pay for it. I'd found the coverage in the fine print, but I missed that there was no guarantee of the cost beyond the three years. Later I learned that the costs typically skyrocketed and became prohibitive. If I had an event relating to the existing aneurysm that was not fatal, he would provide some type of maintenance only if I was 100 percent disabled, i.e., a vegetable, and this arrangement would be put in place only if the disability occurred within the next three years, or within five years from the date of the initial presentation of the aneurysm. After that, any disability that arose from the aneurysm would be solely my responsibility.

One hot August afternoon, I had plans to meet a man named David for coffee at a Starbucks about six blocks from my condo. I'd showered, put on jeans and a T-shirt, done my hair and makeup, and given myself ten minutes to get there. I'd gained some weight; actually, I'd now gained twenty pounds since the thing with Alex ended, but I looked okay. Sort of. I gave Olga a quick pet and a talking to, per the vet's instructions, because Olga suffered from stress-related enterocolitis.

"How can a dog have stress?" I'd asked Jorge, my vet, on the umpteenth visit for Olga's diarrhea. "Do squirrels stress her? Other dogs not playing nice? What?"

"Margaret, it is the stress from your life that is giving your dog colitis. You must sit down with her twice a day and have a nice calming chat. Assure her that everything is okay. Plus try feeding her prescription dog food, make homemade chicken and rice, and put this antibiotic powder on her food. No table food. You know, she's lost weight."

Anyway, Olga lifted one eyebrow as I set off for the coffee shop. Though it wasn't extremely hot yet, it was warm, and humid, and I walked fast, as I always do, because I never leave myself enough time to get anywhere. And as is usually the case, I was a nervous wreck meeting someone new. So by the time I arrived at the Starbucks, all the elements had aligned to form the perfect environment for a hot flash combined with an anxiety attack: humidity, nerves, ambient temperature, elevated heart rate, and hormonal excess. I hit the coffee shop door, sat down, and someone might have turned on a garden hose over my head. The sweat began to pour. My face was drenched. My hair dripped. I looked down, and to my horror, my shirt was soaked through.

Shit. At least David had not yet arrived. That was some good news.

I grabbed a glass of ice water and gulped it down. If anything, I seemed to sweat even more. I took napkins from the dispenser and tried mopping the sweat from my face and neck. So much for makeup. I tried to sneak a discreet look at my armpits.

"Oh my God . . ."

I glanced at the door.

If I left now, would he see me leaving?

This freaking Starbucks was all windows. He'd see me for sure if I bolted now. I'd be a coward. Could I hide in the bathroom for a half hour? Realistically, how long would he wait? I looked around. No! The one Starbucks in America without a restroom!

I'd have to face him. It was simple enough. In today's society we meet psychos all the time. We've come to expect it. I'm not usually at the psycho end of this equation, but there's a first for everything. It might even be my turn! We'd have a cup of coffee, and that would be that. Who in their right mind would ever want to go out with a hormone-addled lunatic anyway? I only had to get through a cup of coffee. I could handle it. Hell, I'd taken years of trauma call! I'd had a brain aneurysm! I could do this!

David walked in the door and came directly over to the table. He shook my sweaty palm. He discreetly wiped his hand on his pants. I wanted to die.

"Can I get you something to drink? A cup of coffee?"

"Actually, I'll take an iced tea," I said, though I'd happily take a short sword on which I might impale myself. "Thank you."

By the time he brought the drinks over, I'd started to cool off, marginally.

"I'm sorry I'm late," David said. "I took my daughter to the airport this morning. Traffic was terrible."

"Oh, not a problem," I said. I just had a small nuclear meltdown that cleared a six-mile radius. No biggie.

"She and her husband were visiting from San Francisco, and they stayed with me for ten days. I miss them when they go, but I finally get back into my own routine. Do you have kids?"

David, it turned out, was older than I'd thought. Stable. Successful. Kind. Really kind. He seemed—this will sound weird, because I had a hard time recognizing it—normal. Not in any rush. He seemed happy with who and what he was. More or less satisfied with his life, though he would like to find a partner. He offered to help me with some family business issues that were tak-

ing up a lot of my time back then, and made some very useful sug-
gestions. He didn't make a single comment about my sweat-soaked
T-shirt.

We had dinner the next weekend. At one point, he leaned across
the table and put his hand on mine and said, "Are you okay?" I never
stopped speaking the entire evening. Nerves, I guess. And then I
never saw him again. I guess I wasn't interested. Or he wasn't interested. Or one of us was just too crazy.

Chapter Twelve

EVERY TIME I go to a fiftieth birthday party, I bring the same gift—a funny card, and a copy of a humor piece by Steve Martin that appeared in the *New Yorker* in January 1998 called, "Changes in the Memory After Fifty." It begins, "Riddle for the over-fifty set: 1. Place your car keys in your right hand. 2. With your left hand, call a friend and confirm a lunch or dinner date. 3. Hang up the phone. 4. Now look for your car keys."

Neal's fiftieth birthday party took place on October 29, 2005, in Northbrook, Illinois, at a remodeled ranch house on a large lot in a wooded part of town. Kate and Neal's old friends hosted the party, and my assignment was to bring a dessert. I stopped at a gourmet grocery in town and picked up a white chocolate mousse cake and some wine, though I knew there would be dozens of desserts and plenty to drink. Most likely, Kate gave the same assignment to many of us. I found a parking spot on the street but sat in my car awhile before getting out and studied the keys in my hand.

I wished I still smoked.

Eventually I emerged from the car, crunched through the leaves to the front door, and let myself in. The house had already filled—at least one hundred people, all of Neal's friends, his bicycling buddies, his dental partners, his neighborhood friends, our work friends, his friends from the school board, many of whom I'd never met.

Neal was recently diagnosed with a malignant brain tumor known as a multifocal glioblastoma multiforme.

Just six weeks earlier I'd walked into a movie theater with a friend when my cell phone rang.

"Honey," Kate's usually cheery voice sounded odd, filled with anxiety, "I need you to do me a favor."

"Sure, anything."

"I'm in Vegas with my cousins, you know, for my birthday. It seems that Neal had a seizure while riding his bike today on the Green Bay Trail. Paramedics took him to Highland Park Hospital. He's in the ER. Would you go up there and see what's going on? I'll take the first plane I can get on, but it will probably be the red-eye."

"Sure, Kate," I said. "I'll leave right now."

I apologized to my friend and left her to see the movie alone.

My mind raced over potentially benign causes of seizures as I drove north.

Hayley and I met Neal and Kate's cousin Derek at the hospital. An ER doc showed us the MRI, already completed by the time I arrived. The MRI demonstrated six lesions on the right side of Neal's brain. Hayley and I immediately saw anxiety in each other's eyes. We both knew what it meant. No benign scenario fit this picture. Neal, a dentist, also knew the MRI did not bode well. We could not reassure him. As much as we wanted to hope, we knew it was not going to turn out all right.

The next week Thomas—our neurosurgeon and friend—biopsied Neal's brain and confirmed the diagnosis.

A glioblastoma multiforme, or GBM as it's often referred to, is one of the worst diagnoses a person can get. And a multifocal GBM, like Neal's, is the worst of the worst. Fifty percent of patients are dead within six months. *Six months.*

We made phone calls and arranged to have Neal see the local expert. We did research and found out who was doing what and where with this type of tumor. Neal began chemo and radiation. Cancer upended their lives. Everything became disarrayed.

Hayley and I struggled to stay positive around them, because Kate and Neal needed hope and positivity. They wanted to remain optimistic, to find a way to face the ordeal of his chemotherapy and radiation and to plan for the time remaining.

But the statistics were abysmal.

When I left Stig, Kate and Neal saved my life. They took care of me, they propped me up, they loved me when I was my most unlovable. I knew they had done the same for other friends, under other circumstances. That alone could have explained the crowd on the occasion of Neal's fiftieth birthday party. I took the cake into the kitchen, then made my way to the bar.

Neal stood in front of the fireplace, head shaved, leaning on a cane, his left side weak from surgery and the tumor, face swollen from corticosteroids, and he started thanking his friends for coming. He had prepared a speech with the understanding that everyone present knew what lay in store for him. I heard his opening lines, declaring his devotion to Kate and to their daughters, thanking them, and thanking his friends for their help. He started to talk about this journey when my phone vibrated. I checked the number and slowly edged toward a bench near the front door. I listened to his self-effacing jokes, heard the laughter in the crowd. Then the applause. Kate and Hayley and I and our husbands cooked together in a group we called Gourmet for years. Neal was like my brother, and like another father to my daughters. I knew his humor well. I thought, He is honest, he is a straight shooter, he is cool. He is a triathlete and a magnificent cook. Two months earlier he competed in an insane bike race in Colorado—the Leadville 100—all above ten thousand feet. Now this. Fuck. I sat on the bench, away from the crowd, to answer my phone. I could still see Neal but could no longer hear him well. The caller ID showed the hospital calling.

"Hello?" I spoke softly into the phone.

The sitter taking care of my mother answered.

"Doctor, honey? It's Josephine. Would you talk to your mama? She's a little confused, talking about that perch thing again . . . I know you just left here." I had spent the day there, in fact. The sitter clucked to my mother, "Now, now, Miss Bonnie. You settle down, honey. I've got your daughter the doctor here."

"Margaret?" my mother shouted into the phone. "Will you come and pick me up? I want to go home. I don't like it here. They're not nice to me."

My mother thought she was a chicken.

On August 20 Mom had fallen into a creek while playing golf at the age of eighty-eight. She was attempting to retrieve a ball from the water. With her ball retriever. Reaching, reaching, reaching— plop she went. Face down.

She did a face-plant in the creek, hitting a rock with her nose. We felt quite lucky she did not lose consciousness and drown.

She managed to scramble out of the creek, and someone called my nearest sister, also named Bonnie, who took her to an emergency care facility, where they did X-rays.

The emergency care facility missed a fracture of her second cervical vertebra, at the upper end of her spine.

They sent her home, bruised, battered, sore, complaining of neck pain.

Three weeks later Mom suffered from chest pains. So she was admitted to the local hospital for a possible heart attack, or what we call a rule-out myocardial infarction.

"You know," Mom said to a nurse once she settled into her room, "my neck still hurts. From that fall three weeks ago."

So someone ordered a CT scan.

Lo and behold, they discovered a fracture of C-2.

The neurosurgeon on staff, who I knew from residency, called and said, "Your mother has an odontoid fracture." That is what this specific type of fracture is called, of the second cervical vertebra. In lay terms, it meant that my mother had a broken neck, although she was neurologically intact, which was the critical factor. We wanted to make certain she did not become paralyzed.

"Was it there on the original films?" I asked, meaning, Did the radiologist miss the fracture when she was first brought in?

"Yes, it was." I appreciated his honesty. To be fair, her neck was filled with arthritis, and the diagnosis of a fracture is not easy in the elderly. But still, they missed the very thing they were looking for.

They put her in a horrendous brace—a custom-made contraption that extended from her lower thorax up to the back of her head and cradled her chin in front—which made her miserable. This was instead of a halo device, with pins in the cranium. Her doctor did not feel an eighty-eight-year-old would tolerate a halo.

He hoped that her broken neck would heal in this immobilizing brace after a month or so. But it didn't.

I had Mom transferred to my hospital, where the surgeons I work with operated on her to stabilize her neck. They performed a posterior cervical fusion at C1-2. She would not be able to drive anymore. And she would no longer be able to play golf. Both of these pissed her off—it's hard to say which pissed her off more. My sisters and I realized that Mom's days of living alone in the house where we grew up had come to an end. We decided to move her into a retirement center where assistance would be available, should she require it. We needed to pack, to organize, to find her a place, to get her used to the idea, to decide what to take, what to sell, what to give away. But the surgery had left her demented. We really really hoped it was a temporary dementia.

"Stop treating me like a chicken! Get me down from this roost!" she cried when I visited her that day.

My normally kind, sweet, funny mother had transformed into a harridan. She swore, viciously, and was meaner than a snake. She talked nonsense; she had completely lost it. I thought, If this is the future, then the future looks grim indeed.

"Doctor, honey? I'm sorry to bother you in the middle of the night . . ."

The phone calls came most nights, at two or three o'clock in the morning, from the nurses and/or the sitters. Though she had been in the hospital two months, it was mostly since the surgery, on October 21, that she had been acting particularly crazy and talking about chickens.

Suddenly, at the hospital that day, I put it all together. The neck immobilizer had disoriented her, disconnected her from her own body.

It made sense, in a strange kind of way. I remembered stories of her childhood, of the farm where she grew up outside Peoria. She used to tell me about watching her brothers kill chickens. She said that the bodies kept moving after the heads had been cut off. Hence the expression, Like a chicken with its head . . .

I tried to put myself in her situation. She lay in bed, unable to turn her head, look up or down. She could only gaze forward, unable to orient herself in space. All she saw lay straight in front of her. To this mix add morphine, old age, a strange environment, sleep deprivation, and macular degeneration, plus some unknown effects of anesthesia in the elderly. We gave her medication to help her sleep, antidepressants, and alternative pain medications (the mechanisms of which we didn't fully understand), as narcotics made her hallucinate. In conclusion, we in medicine have no idea what happens, except it's complicated, and we know it isn't good.

At the hospital, I stood next to her bed and hung her rosary from my hand.

"Mom, see how I am standing up and holding the rosary? See how the rosary is hanging down? Remember gravity? I am standing on the floor." I pointed down to my feet. Then I reached out to the wall. "This is the wall." I pointed up. "This is the ceiling."

"No," she said. "That's the wall." She pointed to the ceiling.

She started to cry. I wanted to cry too.

I started over again. Up. Down. I tried to show her where my feet were.

I felt certain that if she were able to orient herself, she might begin to make sense. I spent the afternoon with her, but most of the time she slept, and I read. She stayed awake at night and slept during the day. The mixing up of the normal diurnal rhythm probably added to her confusion.

When the dinner tray arrived, I faked some enthusiasm, but she gave me her one sane look of the day. A lone slab of ham occupied a plate like a patient in quarantine. Beside it on the tray sat orange Jell-O wrapped in clear plastic. The sight of the Jell-O nearly enraged Mom. She hated it. The corn at least looked edible, though it wasn't. Seriously, is there some reason we cannot feed patients better food? Do we think they would be fighting to stay in the hospital if we gave them good food? What sadist makes this stuff?

As an aside, I've been a patient at this hospital. It's a great hospital. But so I can say, as a heads-up, stay away from the beef broth. I compare it to drinking from the Dead Sea. I have learned to tell all my patients, Whatever you do, don't drink the beef broth. We should probably eliminate the beef broth from the hospital menu, and then check our mortality rate. It might go down.

Someday we'll laugh about this, I thought.

I stopped to see Mom every morning before work, and every afternoon after my cases were finished. I sneaked past the nursing staff—I've worked at or been affiliated with this hospital for a lot of years—because it was hard to admit that this raving lunatic, this screaming nut-bar, was my mom. She was miserable. She was angry. She had no ability to soothe herself. She had no ability to tolerate pain or discomfort. She could not say, I'm lucky to have survived a broken neck. She could not see the big picture.

I love my mom. Where did she go?

After reassuring Mom and the sitter, I hung up the phone and took a sip of wine as laughter brought me back to the present, and the party. Applause broke out—I'd missed most of Neal's speech— and he hugged his wife and daughters. Then Jess, Neal and Kate's younger daughter, stood next to her dad and began speaking.

"Let me tell you about growing up with my dad . . . ," she said, showing her dimples.

Jess started college one month before her dad became ill. She has an adorable smile, dark brown eyes, and thick brown hair. She didn't get it yet—she thought he could beat this thing. The women in the room touched Kleenex to their eyes, the men discreetly sniffed. They knew it could be any of them. They knew it, but they didn't really know it.

My phone vibrated yet again. I looked down. The caller ID told me it was Ruthann calling from New York, where she was in her second year at NYU.

Less than three weeks before Mom's surgery, while driving home from a spinning class at the health club, I'd noticed three messages on my cell phone. Two were from Ruthann. A third message was from a New York number I did not recognize.

I called Ruthie's phone. Her roommate answered.

"Hi, Dr. Overton, it's Elena," she said in a rush. "I'm with Ruthann. We're at Bellevue Hospital, in the emergency room. She's fine, but she's had a little accident. I'll let you talk to her."

"Ruthann?"

"Hi, Mommy. I can't believe I'm such an idiot. I was on Rollerblades. I'm okay, really. Anyway, I'll let you talk to the surgical resident. I messed up my leg, nothing serious, but they want to operate on it, just to clean it up. Here, I'll give the phone to him."

A man's voice came over the phone.

"Dr. Overton, this is Ari Goldman, an orthopedics resident at NYU. Your daughter has road rash on her left inner thigh and right hip, and a traumatic arthrotomy into the left knee joint. We need to do a knee scope tonight to wash it out and make sure there isn't any damage to the cartilage or ligaments in the knee. We'll also clean up the other wounds and dress them. Do we have your permission to do surgery?"

"Yes," I answered. The trauma doctor in me asked the pertinent question first. *Stay calm, lose it later.* "Any head injury, loss of consciousness?"

"No, ma'am. Just the legs. She was lucky. We'll take good care of her. I'll give the phone back to Ruthann."

"I'll be there as soon as I can."

That was a little over three weeks before the party. After Neal's diagnosis, before Mom's surgery.

Ruthann's voice sounded strong over the phone.

"Hey, Mom, whatchu doing?"

"I'm at Neal's birthday party," I spoke quietly into the phone.

"Oh, how is he? Are Marta and Jess there? Say hi to everybody for me. I wish I was there with you."

"I know, sweetie," I said. "I wish you were here too. You can come home anytime you want," I told her. "And I'll be there next weekend."

Ruthann's injuries were horrible, much worse than they had led me to believe over the phone. Then again, they could have been much worse than they were.

While crossing Canal and Broadway on Rollerblades, she tried to hop a curb and slipped. The backs of her blades became wedged in front of the rear wheel of a truck, just as the truck was pulling away from a stop. She grabbed on to the undercarriage of the truck, but it dragged her seventy-five feet or more across an intersection before bystanders were able to get the driver's attention and tell him to stop. Her right hip and left inner thigh and left knee bumped along the ground, tearing away the skin and subcutaneous tissue. An ambulance came quickly, but then the truck driver had to back up in order to free Ruthann's legs from the wheel. The hard plastic of the blades had essentially protected her feet from being crushed by the truck.

When the paramedic got to her, Ruthann looked down at her legs and saw the blood. She started to panic. The EMT removed his hat and put it over her eyes, so that she couldn't see the mess that was her legs, but inside his hat he'd taped a picture of the Virgin Mary. When she saw the image, she really started to panic.

Stig and I took the first plane out of O'Hare in the morning. Stig sat in first class. When we arrived at Bellevue, Ruthann already lay on a cart in the recovery room. Seeing us, she burst into tears.

"Are they giving you enough medicine for pain?" I asked my beautiful baby, my nineteen-year-old baby. I opened my purse— I'd brought along Oxycontin, Vicodin, Tylenol No. 3, Benadryl, and a few other medications, just in case.

The front door opened and latecomers tiptoed into the party. I looked up. My mind snapped back to the present. Ruthie said via phone, "Please tell Neal happy birthday for me, Mom. Tell him I love him, and that I'm thinking of him. Oh, I wanted to tell you—I went to classes this week, on crutches. I took the subway. This city is really not handicapped accessible—it's just terrible. I can't imagine how people who actually are handicapped can live here. But I managed, sort of. Anyway, I'm kind of a celebrity. I think I may to have to drop one class, but I should be able to finish the other three. I've talked to the teachers, and they're going to give me some time to make up what I missed because of the accident. Oh, and I went to that plastic surgeon you found, Dr. Zein—I have to go back twice a week for dressing changes—probably for a month or two. He's really funny, Mom, you'd like him. He yells my name RUTHANN! from one exam room into another—the entire office can hear. He's hysterical, but really gentle. Also Elena has been great. She's a big help—she gets me stuff and helps me with the dressing changes, too. You know her mom's a paramedic, and her grandpa's the fire chief in her hometown."

There I sat, on the bench, phone in hand, just on the periphery of the party. Finally it was Kate's turn to talk. The room grew quiet. Neal stood beside her, an arm around her shoulders. I knew I could not bear to hear what she was going to say. It was too much. As I listened to Ruthann's voice with one ear, and watched Neal and his wife and their children, my phone vibrated again, the hospital calling, yet again. Mom's room. I said good-bye to Ruthann, but the phone stilled, thankfully, and Kate completed her speech to applause. There were no dry eyes left. I sat alone, in the hall, watching Neal. I thought about how people always say that things happen for a reason, but I didn't believe it. We need to think that, to impose some rationalization, some order on a world in which chaos seems to be the only thing we can count on. I've seen too much tragedy, too much awfulness—most medical people have. Chaos, disorder, and complete randomness—that's all we can count on.

It occurred to me that I was in a vortex: three people I loved, from three different generations, with three very different approaches to illness, to life, to the future, were in trouble. Mom had no survival instincts—but a body that would not quit. Neal had all the survival instincts in the world—and a body that had forsaken him. Ruthann, with her strong body and strong instincts for survival, recklessly took them both for granted. I felt the weird harmony of the moment, the synchronicity that seemed enabled by my own brush with death, as if I'd survived the aneurysm to understand this singular moment. How else could I sit here in this foyer in a quiet suburb north of Chicago and take it all in? In some strange, inexplicable way, I came prepared for this exact moment in time, to lend them all support, to be present. I had to laugh—there I was, doing it, too—looking for a reason, when chaos should have been reason enough.

Later that night a group of us sat around a fire in a pit in the yard. My old friend Ben said, "I know exactly what you need, Margaret. You need to get laid."

"I've tried that, Ben. It doesn't work out so well for me," I answered with a smile.

"No, but listen to me. I think you should hire someone."

"Huh?"

"You should hire a gigolo. A prostitute. Someone to have sex with. Pay someone to have sex with."

"Uh, Ben, uh—"

"I know what you're going to say, but before you dismiss the idea, just think about it—keep an open mind. No complications, no messy emotions . . ."

"No matter how desperate I am, I don't see myself paying for sex. But Ben, sweetheart, thanks for thinking of me. I appreciate your concern. If I need any advice in the future, you'll be the last person I ask."

Chapter Thirteen

A week later I walked off a plane at LaGuardia on my way to visit Ruthann and stood face to face with Alex, who was waiting for a flight back to Chicago. I had not seen him in seven months, and my heart clogged my throat.

"What are you doing here?" he asked me.

That seemed a pretty stupid question for a smart guy. He knew my daughter went to school in New York—we'd been there together for a visit.

"Ruthann was in an accident a few weeks ago—" Alex's cell phone rang, and he answered it. He got involved in a lengthy business conversation, and I stood awkwardly, watching him, aware that he had not asked if Ruthann was okay, not sure if I should leave, wait, or what to do. I felt vulnerable, and my face flushed. He looked older to me than he had before.

Just as he ended his phone conversation, a young man in a suit walked up, and said, "Alex!"

"Bart! Good to see you!" Bart reminded me of Christian Bale in the movie version of *American Psycho*.

Alex turned to me, "Margaret, this is Bart. Bart, this is Margaret. Margaret is my proctologist."

I shook my head. I didn't think I'd heard him correctly.

Bart stuck out his hand, and I took it, but my eyes never left Alex. My heart thumped slow and hard.

His proctologist?

"Yeah, Margaret's a doctor, a proctology doctor." Alex didn't look at me. He didn't ask about my daughter. He didn't ask how I was. Nothing.

I turned to Bart. "It was nice meeting you, Bart. I gotta go." I looked one more time at Alex. And then I turned and walked away. Down the long corridor, to the baggage claim, to the taxi stand. To my daughter, to my life, to my responsibilities.

I think, at some level, I realized that I'd just witnessed the single most insensitive act in my entire memory bank, perhaps in my entire life, including the future. And hopefully I had a lot of time left on the clock. But sometimes you just know. Alex had had his defining moment. I called Hayley from the taxi line.

"You won't believe what just happened," I said.

This proctologist did not need another asshole.

But more were to come my way.

"That was really weird, Mom, having you and Dad together for three days. Thank you, though. I know it wasn't easy." Ruthann lay in my bed in the hotel room. She had crutched around the city until she was exhausted. I had spent the weekend on the verge of tears, just looking at her. Changing her dressings caused her terrible pain.

"You don't have to thank me," I said. "Though I gotta say, it was weird being around him. Especially after this summer and the courtroom."

Somehow we had worked out a settlement in late September, after three months of trial.

"Don't tell me about it."

"I wasn't going to."

"Why was it weird?" Ruthann asked.

"'Cause it felt as though he had three years of stored-up stuff he wanted to tell me, so he talked nonstop for three days." And I had felt like an actor, only one without talent. I'd never been so uncomfortable in my life.

"That's funny—he said the same thing about you."

We'd arrived at LaGuardia on the same plane early in the morning after the accident, and as we exited, he asked me if I wanted to share a cab to the hospital. We may never have had much of a marriage to speak of, but now we had everything in common. Seeing Ruthann injured, in pain, wrapped in bandages, encased in the bureaucracy of a public hospital, the two of us worked perfectly in unison. We knew how to take care of her, how to work the system, how to make sure she got adequate care, got the meds she needed, got the blankets, the towels, the antibiotics, the dressings changed, the food she wanted. All hospitals are pretty much the same in fundamental ways. Between the two of us, we'd seen and done it all. What we couldn't do ourselves, we found a way to get done. We were every nurse's worst nightmare. The parents from hell—because we knew exactly what we, and they, were doing. We nagged the shit out of the entire staff. They couldn't wait until we left.

But this is what we do.

Stig had spent five years at a large public hospital. He knew how to cut through red tape to take care of a patient. And I, as an anesthesiologist and a mom, knew how to comfort, knew how to relieve pain, knew how to do everything myself, under the most unusual of circumstances, upside down and backward. So for three days, under unusual circumstances, we were civil to each other, took care of our daughter, and made small talk.

One night Ruthann's friends brought her dinner to the hospital, so Stig and I went across the street for Chinese food.

"You order. You always knew what was best," he said.

I gave our order to the waiter and looked out the window. It had rained every moment since we'd arrived in New York, from Friday morning until now, Sunday night. It felt as if a month had passed, instead of three days, since Elena's phone call.

"So are you dating anyone?" Stig asked me.

"No," I answered. "There was someone, last winter, but it didn't work out."

"I'm sorry, Margaret."

"Yeah, me too."

"Was that the guy with the Maserati? I saw the car when you picked up Olga that time." Stig occasionally took Olga when I traveled.

"Yeah."

"Maseratis always made you carsick anyway."

"I know."

"Probably best it didn't work out."

"Before I puked in his hundred-thousand-dollar car, you mean?"

"Right."

We both nodded.

"How's your mom?"

"She has a broken neck," I said. "Broke it golfing. Put her second shot into the creek—"

"Was that on number four? The dogleg left on the blue nine?" I never understood how he could have memorized every hole of my parents' country club golf course but not remember my birthday or our anniversary.

"No, I think it was somewhere on the red nine. I'm not sure. Anyway, she had her ball retriever out and was fishing in the water after her ball . . ." I explained the mechanism of Mom's fracture and subsequent hospitalization to Stig.

"So things are going well," he said, nodding. And the thing was, he meant it.

"You mean, besides Neal having a brain tumor?" *And after the month I spent in court with you this summer?*

"I'm sorry to hear about that."

The dinner passed easily enough. We had twenty-five years of friends and family in common, and three plus years had passed since we'd spoken to any extent. He talked about his mother's death the year before, and about how his father was coping. Stig seemed almost normal again.

But a couple of weeks later I got a phone call from my attorney. Stig had reneged on the settlement. There would be no divorce this year.

Mom left the hospital a few days before Thanksgiving.

"You thought you were a chicken," I told her, smiling. I thought she might laugh. My mother, once upon a time, had had a remarkable sense of humor. Wicked. Slightly mean.

"I did not," she answered. She was not laughing, nor was she smiling, and she had no plans to start. We sat in her new kitchen, at the new table and chairs that Erica and I had picked out, which fit perfectly, which matched everything, and which Mom hated. She hated her new condo in the retirement community we'd chosen for her, where her older sister (ninety-five, deaf, no sense of humor) also lived. She hated wearing her neck brace. She hated the surgeon for telling her she had to wear it. She hated the food at the retirement community. She hated the view. She hated not driving. She hated me for transferring her to the hospital where she had had the surgery that resulted in all the changes in her life, because everything had been fine until she'd come to the hospital where I had worked. She forgot about the important stuff, like breaking her neck. She missed her house. Who could blame her? She'd missed the end of the golf season, which was also my fault. She couldn't find anything at the new condo. She didn't like the people at the retirement community. They stole from her. They weren't friendly.

"Why am I here?" she asked constantly. "When am I going home? And who took my car?"

We invited Neal and Kate and their daughters to our house for dinner the night after Thanksgiving.

Ruthann sat on a barstool in the kitchen, while Bea grated cheese for the lasagna and I cooked the Italian sausage.

"You know, it's one thing to lose your dad because he's got a brain tumor," Ruthie said. "It's horrible, and sad. But when your dad just goes off with someone else and doesn't want to be part of the family anymore, it really sucks. And you still have to deal with him, even though he's an asshole."

"Shut up Ruthie," Bea said. "It's not like he's dead."

We glanced at each other then, and turned away, uncomfortable with our thoughts. It would have been easier if he were dead. No one wanted to say it out loud. We had places to set and a salad to toss.

Neal was still doing pretty well, at that point, still conversant, mostly upbeat, but I suspected it would be the last time he came to our house. After they left, Bea and Ruthie and I got into my bed and watched *Home for the Holidays* together, then fell asleep.

In December, Ruthann told me she wasn't going back to school after Christmas break.

"I can't, Mom. I've hit the wall," she said. She wanted to go to bed, and she wanted to stay there. She needed time off, she told me. One semester, maybe more. I realized what I'd been too pre-occupied to see: Ruthann had had her own near-death experience to cope with. Burdened with more than just physical scars and two healing legs, she had to walk the same path I'd recently taken, and was still taking. But she was only nineteen years old. If I found it isolating, imagine how difficult it was for her.

"Okay," I said. "But I expect you to get a job. Write. Do some-thing."

In early January 2006 my attorney called to inform me that all the court documents in my case had been lost. Although some of the record could be re-created, we would have to go back to court. And I would have to take more time off from work. I was already down several hundred thousand dollars in legal fees.

I thought he was kidding. It felt like a huge joke. I could not believe it.

I flew to New York for my old friend Rae's fiftieth birthday week-end. She'd come up from Memphis with her friend Susie from

Muscle Shoals, Alabama. The three of us stayed at Rae's brother's house in Brooklyn for a few days in celebration of the big event.

At O'Hare, on the way home from New York, I had another moment of clarity. It hit me as I walked through the airport on a snowy Sunday evening in January. I literally stopped, in the middle of the airport terminal. I knew what I had to do. I had to finish the divorce. I had to give up. I could not fight any longer—it was going to kill me. I only had so much energy, I'd been functioning on reserve power for months, and Ruthann and Mom and Neal needed whatever energy I had left. I could not handle one more thing. They were more important than slugging it out in court. Money didn't matter anymore—Stig was going to make sure I spent more in legal fees than anything I'd get in a settlement. I would apply for the state health insurance, or else find a job with coverage. I would be working until I dropped dead anyway, if I was lucky. If I was really lucky, I would work all day, go home, drop dead, and not stop for groceries first. I would die with an empty tank of gas.

I called my attorney Adam from the airport. I left him a message.

"Do whatever you have to do to finish this now. I give in. Give him whatever he wants. I have to be done. You can call me tomorrow."

Within two weeks I walked out of Adam's office a free woman. I went home, put the Stones on the stereo, and played air guitar to "Start Me Up."

Ruthann proceeded to do what any nineteen-year-old who had just had a near-death experience would do: she found a group of kids to party with. She stayed out most nights, slept all day, smoked, watched TV, seemed depressed, refused to go to therapy, and sometimes didn't change out of her pajamas for three days at a time. Her

lethargy worried me. At some point she developed an orbital cellu-
litis—a dangerous infection around her eyeball—which I treated
with antibiotics. I put an IV in her and kept it there for three days,
giving her vancomycin every eight hours until it seemed safe to put
her on oral meds.

I tried to get over to see Neal once a week. With each visit, his
left side grew weaker, his face became puffier from the massive
doses of steroids he took to control the brain swelling, and he grew
more depressed. Sometimes he wouldn't talk at all. Sometimes I went
along to see the oncologist, to act as another set of "ears."

One afternoon I sat with Kate and Neal in their living room
with Hayley and a few other visitors. Neal had had chemo that
week. He could not get comfortable. He was nauseated. He was
anxious. He was irritable. He wanted company, he wanted to be
alone. He wanted food, he wanted to throw up. He wanted to sit,
he wanted to lie down. He was hot, he was cold. He wanted the
blanket on, he pushed it to the floor. He felt like dying. He didn't
want to die. Finally I caught Kate's eye and brought my thumb
and forefinger to my mouth. I pursed my lips. And inhaled.

Neal, unlike some other people, needed to get high.

Kate nodded and left the room.

Why do we make it so fucking difficult for patients to obtain
marijuana?

Neal had to get it from friends of his college-age kids.

It is the ideal drug for chemotherapy patients. Nothing compares.
Anyway.

Chapter Fourteen

MY THERAPIST RECENTLY referred to me as the adult in the room. He said I've always been the adult in the room, from childhood on.

This did not apply to my love life.

So while I was in this vortex, this cauldron of emotional need and sadness, I found a guy on Match.com. His name was Max. But in my mind I don't think of him as Max. I think of him as Max, the Min Man.

The thing I liked best about Max was his name. And that he was handsome in a somewhat dissipated way. He reminded me of an Irish, redheaded version of Omar Sharif in *Funny Girl*, but after the prison stint. We had nothing in common.

Max said he'd trained to be an attorney but hated practicing law. He worked as a commercial butcher instead. He owned his own shop—an upscale "boutique" from which he sold the meat of dead animals that had spent their brief lives freely grazing the fertile fields of Spartan midwestern states. Prized clients included trendy restaurants specializing in locally grown comfort food. In his spare time he wrote vaguely pornographic freeform verse that he considered a metaphor for his disinterest in commitment. He believed in content over structure, preferring inmates to institutions.

I'd found a man of metaphor.

The other thing I liked about Max was that I didn't really like him at all. I enjoyed his sense of humor but I didn't particularly respect him. This led me to believe that I would not actually fall for him. Max appealed to me precisely because he had never grown up, never matured, never become responsible. He espoused animal rights but treated people with disdain. A part of me wanted to be that kind of person too—the hell with ethics or consistency! I wanted to be someone else, someone thirty years younger, someone without accountability who could just walk away as if no one depended on me. If I hung out with Max, I could pretend I was young and in college and having fun, with no one but myself to care for. I'd lost interest in love, conceptually. It didn't pay. So I liked Max rather tangentially. He attracted me precisely because I knew the relationship would not go anywhere.

Max had a lot of opinions, but they all regarded topics about which I could not care less. He railed, even pontificated, about the moral ineptitude of *Seinfeld*, for example, but told me he'd had a secret affair for years while he lived with a woman. I loved that! His principles were highly flexible. Unformed. Immature. *Seinfeldian*.

I never followed his rationale about the sitcom. I believe far worse televised sins have been perpetrated on the American public. What about *Married . . . with Children*? Besides, wasn't moral ineptitude the whole point of *Seinfeld*?

Max tried to pigeonhole me, to figure me out. He said, "I know, you're a folkie," meaning, he thought I liked folk music, which I do, but in minuscule doses. I like all types of music—jazz, rock, opera, pop. But not hip-hop. He saw my house and said, "You're a minimalist." I smiled. Divorce brought that on. He thought I should enjoy the things he enjoyed such as birding and paddle tennis and building complex origami projects. I enjoyed them until I didn't. He never asked about my interests.

Max liked to hold forth. My sister Beth came to visit, met Max, and instantly hated him. His arrogance pressed her mute button. She would not even sit in the same room with him. I had to walk from one room to the next and back to have a conversation with the two of them.

Beth sees things clearly—black and white. I see all shades of gray.

The first time I saw Max's house, it thrilled me. He had appallingly bad taste, and he hoarded, in contrast to my minimalism. He may never have thrown anything out. Ever. Newspapers, magazines, furniture from college, clothes from late adolescence. Not cool period stuff. Just ugly, and lots of it. I liked that about him. It reinforced my belief that our relationship was doomed.

He said he kept in close contact with his inner child. That child expressed itself in verse which I adroitly avoided reading. Max claimed to be completely self-taught. And I believed him.

"Wow," I said when he read a poem to me, when I could not avoid his creative output a moment longer. "That is really something." I used a trick I'd learned in high school: how to appear interested and evasive at the same time.

For his birthday, I bought him a Zen drawing board. You draw, and your drawing disappears as it dries. It seemed apropos. Everything about Max felt temporary. Or more accurately, that was how I felt about Max.

After a couple of months, I realized Max's marginal attachment to me was the only constant and predictable thing about him. The rest of Max was fluid, adaptable. He took off at a moment's notice. Nothing about my life experience to that point could relate, but I admit to having been a tad jealous of the freedom afforded by his mental agility. I was thoroughly stuck in the here and now. Pain secured me like quicksand. Despite my best efforts, I just couldn't leave it behind.

"You don't seem to know how accomplished you are," Max said to me. "Or how powerful." I had no response to that. I supposed he was right.

We dated off and on. Not long after I started seeing Max, Neal died. In early March.

In the synagogue, I stood between my two girls, an arm around each of them as we listened to the many testimonials to Neal. How hard he'd fought. How much he'd been loved.

Bea rested her head on my shoulder, crying silently. "With Dad, it was voluntary," she said. "He didn't fight for us."

Ruthann asked, "Why do the good ones always die?"

They felt Neal's loss very personally, as if they'd lost their own father all over again. It was somehow harder this time. It did not seem right, or fair.

I thought back to the morning in the bedroom. "Fine," Stig had said.

Divorce feels like death to kids. But they don't get the sympathy.

Bea and Ruthie and I spent the evening at Kate's house. We held each other. We hugged Kate's daughters, our other friends, and her family, ate, drank, cried, and sat on the sofa, on the floor, nestled into chairs with Kate's aunts and cousins and Hayley and Daniel and their kids and the women from work. We took vicarious comfort from the warmth and the support. It felt unbearably sad.

A new boyfriend seemed particularly meaningless now that I was grieving. He lacked relevance and context, or at least Max did. The world had shifted, and grief was the anchor. Max would call, we would talk. He tried. I came up against the ineffectiveness of language, the emptiness of words. "Describe Neal for me," Max said. And I couldn't. It seemed gratuitous. Why describe him to someone whom he'd never get to know? Why try to summarize a man in words—when words aren't up to the task, when I wasn't up to the task? I could describe how wrong it felt, the hollowness he'd left in his absence. But I could not—for the life of me—describe Neal.

It struck me as absurd that some people got high because life wasn't intense enough to hold their attention, but Neal got high because life had become too intense. I could barely stand the irony.

You see, I wanted what they'd had—what Kate and Neal had shared. I wanted that kind of love. I didn't want to date a man like Max, who seemed not to appreciate me or anything else of value in his life; or another Alex, who pawed me in public, then withdrew in private; or another Nikolaos, who was just plain creepy; or another Nigel, who wanted to possess a woman instead of love one. I wanted to find a good man, a man with values like mine, who understood that life is a gift and knew how not to squander it. I wanted—want—to find a man who understands that life is not a series of endless tomorrows, who tries—like I do now—not to fuck up even one single day.

But all I could find were men like Max—men who made an issue of trust when they were untrustworthy themselves. All I could

find were men who got high making money and had disconnected
their hearts from the rest of themselves. I found men who avoided
intimacy. I found men who avoided life.

In May, I took Mom to Arkansas for Rae's mother's ninetieth
birthday party. My phone rang just before takeoff.

"Mom, I have some awful news," Bea said, crying. "Dad just
called." Two more good friends had died that spring weekend.
Soni and Bob, old neighbors who had lived downstairs during my
anesthesia residency, who had taught me everything I know about
antiques and peach pies and making a dirty martini, had been killed
in a car accident while vacationing in France. Soni had loaned me
Laura Ashley dresses when I was pregnant with Bea, loaned us a
coffee table when we couldn't afford one. And now they were gone.
Just like that. In a heartbeat.

That summer I had migraines for weeks at a time. I had a visual
aura every single day. Josh did another angiogram, but he said the
aneurysm looked stable. There were days I felt as though I couldn't
breathe.

Ruthann moved back to New York, to continue school and work.
Bea moved into an apartment of her own. I found myself alone again.

One Tuesday that September, after eight months of on-and-off
dating, Max called to break up with me over the phone. It was September 19, 2006, to be precise, three days before I was to leave for a
bike trip through the Burgundy region of France. The conversation
was brief, cell phone to cell phone, and we actually had a good con-
nection, though I was driving through an area on the northwest side
of Chicago with lots of forest preserves and poor cell coverage. For
once, I understood every word he said.

"Remember I told you about that other person I'd been involved with for years? Well, she's come back into my life, and I need to find out what's there."

My heart went into that slow dull thud that it does when it hears news like this. My face felt hot—seared, actually. Like tuna in a nice restaurant. Cold on the inside, hot on the outside. It wasn't the first time I'd felt this way. I was used to these words, but not used to the feeling. I didn't even like Max, but rejection hurts because it's supposed to.

"Did you think about how you'd hurt me?" In that moment, I'd become expendable, disposable. I thought about the song John C. Reilly sings in the musical *Chicago*, "Mr. Cellophane." That was me. See-through, dissolving.

"I thought about it all weekend." That wasn't very long to think, which meant that he'd slept with her first, then thought about me later. What a predictable prick.

"Is she there now?" I asked. You think you can prevent this from happening. Somehow, if you're careful enough, you can prevent yourself from getting hurt. But it isn't true. It can happen even when you don't love him.

"No," he answered. I'd calculated that Max was the seventeenth man I'd met on Match.com, and I'd hoped he'd be the last. I was sick of it all. Perhaps I'd gotten used to him. He'd become convenient. I liked having a boyfriend who never came to my house; I could visit him when I wanted. I didn't love him, and I hadn't wanted to, so it surprised me how much it hurt. "She came to visit last weekend."

"You were with me on Thursday," I said. Thursday night. "And you knew she was coming to visit?" I started looking for somewhere to pull over. I needed to pull the car over. Quickly. I had to vomit. "Jesus Christ." I hung up. I stopped the car and opened the door, but not in time.

The day after the phone conversation, he sent me an e-mail, titled "An Expla(i)nation." As if it expla(i)ned anything.

I felt a grief completely out of proportion to my feelings for Max. At best, those feelings were tepid. I mean I had read that poetry! But it represented another failure on my part. I felt terrible. Lonely and depressed.

It occurred to me along the way that loss is cumulative. It chips away at your heart, making it harder and harder to mend.

One of the rhetorical questions that people ask (though I hate these types of discussions) is whether I think that heartache—over a certain age—is worse than when you're a kid. I always used to answer the same way: how do you compare pain? But the question had begun to take on a distinctly personal tone, and I recognized that the problem was that loss doesn't occur in a vacuum. It occurs in the middle of an already-complicated life, a life filled with other types of loss, and financial problems, and job worries, and parents who might be elderly or infirm or have dementia, and kids with school problems, or drug problems, or depression. When you're young, heartache makes you feel as if the world will end. When you're older, you know it won't. Unfortunately, you know exactly what that means.

I tried to rationalize the extent of my grief. I should be angry. Instead I felt down. I hadn't even liked Max. But being with him made me feel like I could pretend I was still young and entitled to hope, before I'd made so many mistakes. I could pretend I'd started all over—that this was someone else's life. I could go to his awful house, and be someone who didn't have any worries. That part was fun. And I was sorely in need of some fun. But in the end I couldn't even maintain a relationship that I didn't want. So how would I ever maintain a relationship that I did want? Did it make a difference?

I focused my grief on Max, unfairly, but my grief was manifold, and the losses were beginning to mount. Nurse Barb, Neal, Soni and Bob, all gone in less than a year's time. Ruthann's accident, my mom's accident. Finalizing the divorce. The grief, the stress, the burden of my aneurysm with the attendant uncertainty of my own future, it all began to take its toll.

Less than a week after the Max incident, I left for a cycling vacation in Burgundy with my old friend Ben. Unfortunately, I brought myself along.

Ben and I left Chicago for Paris on a Friday night. Rain delayed our flight, so we spent hours in O'Hare getting drunk and playing Hot Or Not with all the men who wandered past the bar. Ben's taste at the time ran to young slacker dudes, whereas I tended to pick out middle-aged men who looked employed. Wall Street types. But nobody seemed all that appealing. I realized I had no idea what kind of man I liked. Did I like men?

We arrived in Paris the next day, feet swollen, bleary eyed, and hung over, and stowed the bags at our hotel. We went to see an exhibition of Marilyn Monroe photographs by Bert Stern at Musée Maillol. Stern had taken the photos shortly before Monroe's death in 1962. In one photograph she was nude, but for silk flowers covering her breasts. Her gallbladder scar appeared fresh and angry, in contrast to her face, which she had turned aside. I bought posters for Bea and Ruthann.

Ben and I ate an early dinner at a small bistro in the Marais recommended by a friend from Chicago. Except for a single man alone at a table near the door, we were the only people in the restaurant. The man came over and asked, in English, if he could join us. He introduced himself as Dino, explained that he was also from Chicago, and said he was the French wine buyer for a large wine shop—of course we'd heard of it—where we both bought our wine! He'd been touring vineyards for three weeks and was longing for some American companionship. He tasted so much wine, visited so many vineyards, he explained, that by the end of three weeks he had a serious acid burn on his tongue. While he talked, I imagined myself drowning in a vat of wine. Voluntarily.

I'd worried that Ben might be a difficult travel partner, picky, or a complainer. Instead, I quickly found him to be relentlessly cheerful, adaptable, and even fluent in French. He easily made conversation with nearly everyone, read signs, and laughed good-naturedly at my poor attempts at the language. He was, in many ways, an ideal travel partner. The next morning we took the TGV train to Dijon and met the biking group at the station. Our group consisted of two other singles, the rest couples, for a total of twenty people, including two female guides. Ben and I fell right in the middle of the age range—early forties to mid-fifties—and most everyone seemed friendly, fit, and interested in wine. The trip would take us through the heart of the Burgundy wine region, featuring stops at vineyards for educational purposes as well as tasting and buying. We would eat at a couple of Michelin one-star and two-star restaurants.

The French countryside in autumn inundated the senses with fragrances. In addition to the ubiquitous cow poop, I detected lavender, fermenting grapes, shallots, and more lavender. I smelled fennel. I stopped, I sniffed. Yes, there was the ever-present meth-ane, but the French cows seemed so soigné in repose. I took their pictures. Just for a moment, I caught a scent, an evanescence, that summoned a memory, something fleeting, a warmth, some brief time perhaps when I was not—so—fucking—miserable—and—alone. But isn't being alone essentially the human condition?

Soni and Bob had died in France. They had been together, at the end.

Neal had died surrounded by his loved ones.

I have got to stop feeling sorry for myself. I am not alone. I have friends and family who love me. I love them. Many people don't even have that. Maybe my kids are the loves of my life. I must try to reorient myself. Maybe that is the great lesson I am supposed to learn—that my love for Bea and Ruthann is the emotional fulfillment I've been crav-ing, and it has been there all along.

Those were my thoughts, while I was biking.

Why did I feel so alone? Why did I obsess about dying alone?

I had been to hundreds of codes—or "code blues," as they're called on television. And by and large, people who die in the hos-pital, they do it alone. Maybe that's a select group. Maybe I'm see-ing a select group. Maybe most people are luckier.

But the passage itself, it is not something you share. It's a trip you take by yourself. Whether or not you love someone, or whether or not someone loves you, in the end, you make that journey your own.

Don't you?

Those were my thoughts while I rode. I was a freaking morose freak of nature.

Death.

Death.

Being alone. Death.

We stayed in picturesque hotels, startlingly lovely, with breath-taking views, and I remained nearly catatonic. I wrote in my journal, long self-pitying entries that bored the crap out of me when I reread them. Get a grip! Ben cheerfully dragged me to dinner each night, and out for drinks afterward, but my misery and self-pity accompanied me like a thick, comfy sweater, one that stank of age and overuse. I might have been the first person ever to suffer a broken heart after being dumped by someone I didn't even like. Or maybe my heart was just broken from having been through too much.

On the third day we biked along the Route de Grand Crus and stopped for a picnic lunch at the Cuvée Municipale in Meursault. Our guides had set out the lunch on two long tables with wonderfully stinky cheeses from the region, fresh baguettes, grapes and apples. They encouraged us to eat before going into the wine-tasting room, so that we didn't get shit-faced drunk before getting back on our bicycles. Our charming, perky blonde guides, Annette and Paula, did not explain it exactly this way.

As I approached a table, I heard one of the cyclists, Ellen, a psychologist, say, "Fifty percent . . ."

Ellen and her husband both came from Philadelphia, where Ellen had a private practice but also taught at a prominent business school. Her husband Kevin ran a not-for-profit in the city. They seemed warm and genuine, and I liked them.

"Fifty percent of what?" I asked, butting into the conversation.

"We were discussing happiness," Ellen said, and my ears perked up. As a miserable person, I could use a few pointers on happiness. I could be a student of happiness. Currently an expert on its antithesis, I wanted to hear what Ellen had to say.

She looked up and down the picnic table at the brightly dressed bikers, some sitting, some standing, some still in helmets. The table was strewn with our paraphernalia—gloves, water bottles, sunglasses—in addition to the food. Ellen wore her gray hair short, but her face looked young. She took in our group, but I felt as if she were speaking directly to me.

"There's a lot of evidence that suggests fifty percent of happiness is determined by genetic predisposition, or your 'set point.'

"When things happen, good things, bad things, you win the lottery, you lose a spouse, there might be a significant time period of perturbation of the baseline, but eventually most people return right back to their set point. This has been repeatedly shown in research, particularly in regard to the popular conception that the pursuit of money leads to happiness. We tend to think that if we just get this new job, or a raise, our lives will improve. And they do, briefly, but then they return right back to baseline. This concept is referred to as 'hedonic adaptation,' which is a great phrase, I think. Money really does *not* buy happiness."

Jed, a Texas dentist, volunteered, "Maybe not, but it makes being unhappy much more comfortable."

Murmurs of assent came from around the table.

"Anyway," Ellen continued, "so fifty percent of our happiness is determined by the set point. That leaves about ten percent to be determined by circumstances, and about forty percent of happiness is purely volitional, or a result of the choices we make."

The numbers generated lots of discussion. Being a math person, I had trouble believing that only 10 percent of happiness was a result of happenstance. What about Holocaust survivors? People who'd lost children? It seemed impossible. Life's really big perturbations seemed capable of taking a bigger chunk than 10 percent.

I thought of my own recent past.

But Ellen went on. "Interestingly, the evidence suggests that there are things you can do to raise your set point. Specifically, three things.

"One is to regularly say thank you to people who are an important part of your life, or who have given you something, even if it is an intangible. Saying thank you, showing appreciation, actually has been shown to make you happier. Doing it in writing is even better. Something about documentation that seals it.

"Another is to count your blessings, to remind yourself of what's good in your life.

"And the third is to regularly reassess what you want to accomplish in life—say, every six months—and make an effort to take steps to do so. If you want to travel more, plan a trip. If you want to learn a language, sign up for a class. The point is, don't procrastinate. Set goals for yourself, and follow through. You'll feel a sense of accomplishment, and that increases happiness. Hence the concept of the 'bucket list.'"

A few people asked Ellen questions, then wandered inside. I sat at the table long after everyone else left to taste wines. I tried to take it all in. I could not believe there was actual scientific data, hard numbers, actual research to document what made people happy! Practically a formula! But only 10 percent due to circumstances? That didn't seem possible! And yet I felt as though I'd been handed the keys to something critically important. After a few minutes, I rushed to my bicycle, grabbed my journal, and started writing. I wrote down everything that Ellen had said. I couldn't wait to get home and start doing research. I couldn't wait to read the original articles. And then I thought: Max doesn't count his blessings! Max doesn't appreciate me! Max doesn't say thank you! Max has totally fucked his own set point!

Yup, that's what I thought. Someone should have smacked me in the head. *God* should have smacked me in the head.

Actually, God *had already* smacked me in the head, and I had not learned a single thing. God should have knocked me off my bicycle, taken away my journal, and then done a full body tackle.

After the bike trip, we took the train back to Paris, and Ben departed for Spain. I had two days by myself before flying home. The ladies at the hotel desk gave me detailed instructions on how to use the Paris Metro, and so I went underground to find Le Bon Marché, my late friend Soni's favorite store, where I bought presents for both daughters, and wrinkle cream for myself. Then I took the Metro to Notre Dame. I had found a Web site with a self-guided tour of little-known architectural points of interest inside and outside the great cathedral that could be completed in three hours, and I'd printed it out. In memory of my mom's experience as a chicken, I made a point of finding headless Saint Denis (aka Dionysius) near the main doors and taking his picture. Then I walked along Rue de Fauburg Saint Honoré, and bought myself a purse, and shoes, and a sweater, and a pair of jeans. I spent a lot of money and had great fun doing it. Despite speaking little to no French, I found Parisians to be very friendly. My sweater was very elegant. And my jeans were very tight.

That night I went to a party. It happened that a friend from Chicago was spending a week in Paris for the occasion of her six-tieth birthday. And so she invited me to attend. I knew no one except the birthday girl and her husband. It did not matter.

I left the party at two A.M., very drunk. In retrospect, I should have thought to have the restaurant call a taxi. But I did not. I stumbled out into the streets of Paris, with no idea where I was, so I wandered about, this way and that, looking for something that seemed familiar.

I had the vague idea that I would take the Metro home, now that I was a veteran Metro rider, with a total of one day's experience. I did not realize that the Metro closes at midnight.

I could not find a taxi stand. I ventured farther afield, but I had no idea what part of Paris I was in. I wandered farther still. And became more lost. *Lost-er?* Is that a word? This began to concern me, since I had to leave for the airport at seven A.M.

I was looking a lot less like the adult in the room. More like Saint Denis, but without the Saint part.

Eventually a taxi let two people out, and I jumped in. The driver took pity on my predicament and drove me to my hotel, which was, I think, about ten miles away.

I made my plane. By some miracle, or perhaps through a prayer to a saint who had also lost his head, American Airlines randomly upgraded me to first class so that I could sleep off my hangover in extreme comfort.

A couple of weeks after I got home from Paris, I woke up one morning, and clarity struck. Out of the blue, as usual. Max had never been what I wanted. I'd just wanted him to want me. And when he didn't, it hurt. I was lucky I didn't spend twenty years with him before I figured it out.

And with that, I got over it, and him. He became Max, the Min Man.

Chapter Fifteen

I LOOKED UP the research Ellen mentioned and read extensively in the field of positive psychology. I spent many hours online reading full texts of articles and found it surprising how much work had originated in the field of economics. It makes sense, I guess, that economists would want to know what causes happiness, so that they could understand what drives market forces. I read the works of Nobel Prize winner Daniel Kahneman, a prolific researcher and pioneer in the field of hedonic psychology, and of Ed Diener, a professor at the University of Illinois who's written extensively on positive psychology.

But as much as I searched, I did not find the statistics of which Ellen spoke. The papers describing the "easy resetting of the 'set point' by saying thank you, counting your blessings, periodically evaluating your goals in life" eluded me. The 50/40/10 concept. Believe me, I searched.

But it occurred to me, eventually and after much reading, that I had missed Ellen's point completely. I had within me, we all have within ourselves, the capacity to be happy. It is not an entitlement. Sometimes it's work. Some days it comes more naturally than others.

But it requires a basic acknowledgment of the input of other people into our lives—that in and of itself is a personality trait. It even explains, I think, why narcissists tend to be unhappy. They're self-centered. They don't take other people into consideration. Not others' input, nor the effect they have on others.

I thought about Ellen's assessment. I already wrote thank-you notes, I wrote to people all the time. Often long, heartfelt letters, because I believe that receiving handwritten messages is one of life's great joys. But wallowing in my own misery—ruminating on the bad stuff—which I also did, may not be productive in the long run. In the short run, perhaps it helps to work things out. But long-term rumination wasn't going to do me any good. Did I count my blessings? I gave myself an F in that. And as for my bucket list, that would take some thought. Something started to rumble inside me. I didn't yet know what it was.

Back when I was married, and my kids were young, and I had a house, with a yard, I could keep busy. I could garden. Or cook. Or pick up a few extra days at work. Or clean out the kids' closets, or drawers, or my closets or drawers. Or write short stories about ways to kill off my husband.

But the kids were gone. The husband was an ex. I had no one to cook for.

Divorce had turned me into a minimalist. I had been cleaned out, there was nothing left to clean. I had a condo—i.e., no yard.

I was technically an employee of my group, not a partner, and my days were too short. I didn't work enough hours.

I did a couple of projects for some guys who had a consulting business, but it really wasn't my thing. I knew it, and they knew it.

I already exercised obsessively so that my joints hurt in equal measure. I had to rotate activities; step aerobics, dance aerobics, spinning, swimming, power walking, etc.

And then something bad happened. Boredom set in. Boredom proved to be a very dangerous thing for me.

So—I—went—back—on—Match—dot—com. I groan as I write this. Because you would think by now that I would have learned that a man was not the answer. Wouldn't you? But I had not yet learned that lesson. I honestly didn't know what the answer was, but friends and family kept telling me that it was just a matter of time. I would find him. It seemed so clear to everyone that I was not meant to be single. So I searched, out of loneliness, out of some ingrained belief that I could not be happy alone.

And I met a man named Mitchell. An attractive attorney, fifty years old. He'd been married years before, then had lived with a woman for a few years and had moved out six months earlier. One grown son. He had the best clothes of any man I'd ever met. And he smelled good. Nice-looking, educated, funny, self-effacing, well spoken, he seemed like a complete gentleman. On our first date, we had a drink, then dinner, and we hit it off immediately.

"I love your e-mails," he said, smiling. "They are extremely funny."

On our second date, we went to dinner and a play.

He said, "We may be the only two people in North America who haven't seen *Chicago*."

He was a trifle stodgy, but otherwise lovely. Maybe stodgy would be good for me, instead of boorish and overbearing. Stodgy beats a man in makeup any day. Stodgy certainly seemed a marked improvement over cheating scumbags, hands down! Stodgy could, in fact, if looked at in just the right light, be the whole package.

In our six-week courtship, I saw Mitchell (his name was actually Mitchell, not Stodgy) several times a week. I met his family, and he met my family. And then one evening, shortly after Thanksgiving, I asked him directly about his ex-girlfriend, and he clammed up, said he wasn't sure it was really over. He'd heard from her, and things seemed "too good, too perfect" with me, that nothing should actually be "that perfect," and he walked out of my apartment.

I never heard from him again.

I took the third strike, and I was out.

I slid into a depression that held on to me tight, threatened me, pulled me deeper than I'd ever gone. I could not see the light. I thought, for the first time in my life, about suicide. I'm lucky it did not last long. Had it not been for my daughters, for my responsibility to them, for my responsibility to my stressed-out Olga, had something easy come along, had I been in the right place at the right time, I might have let go. It's hard to tell what might have been. My despair felt interminable.

Maybe it was because of the aneurysm, because I was still alive after all of that. Maybe it was because of the lights in the park at night, blinking frantically at me. Maybe it was because of a particularly pristine winter night when a fresh coat of snow covered Lincoln Park, when I stood under one light and it turned on and off, and on and off. I knew something had to change. I knew I could not continue doing what I'd been doing. Something about me had to change. I had selected the wrong path. For the first time in years, I prayed. I prayed to God to help me get through this. And I dragged myself to Mass. Week after week. And slowly, incrementally, I found a way out of the despair.

At some point I realized that I could count on myself, on my kids, on my friends, and on my family. And I recognized that I needed to put my efforts into myself. I needed to stop looking for a man to complete me. Isn't that what I'd been doing? I had taken my career and my God-given talents for granted long enough. Max was right about that. I didn't know how accomplished I was. It was time to take stock, to count my blessings, to recognize where my talents lay, and to give them their due. It was time to say thank you.

I found a Catholic church in Chicago—a radically progressive Jesuit parish filled with disillusioned Catholics like myself—and I started going every week. I found one magnetic priest I liked, and I went to his Mass every Sunday at eleven-fifteen. I wore dark glasses and cried through every Mass. I have a messy relationship with religion. I believe in God, but I find organized religion too excluding and dogmatic.

One Saturday evening I took a taxi to Holy Name Cathedral, not my usual church. My Muslim cabdriver asked about my Catholicism. Our eyes met in the rearview mirror.

"I'm a bad Catholic," I answered. "I'm not even sure I'm a Christian."

"Then why do you go to Mass?" he asked.

"I was raised Catholic, so it's comforting. I like the ritual. And I go to pray."

"What do you pray for?" He looked at me in his rearview mirror. "I'm interested. My wife's not Muslim, she's Presbyterian. She won't convert because she doesn't want to give up pork."

"I'm a physician," I told him. I glanced at his registration. "Nabil. I pray for my patients. I pray that I won't harm anyone."

"Do you want to know what I think?" Nabil asked me.

"Yes."

"I think Jesus Christ was a prophet. But I do not think he was the son of God. Because I do not believe God would let his son be tortured that way."

"Many people would agree with you," I said. "I'm not certain what I believe, except that he lived an exemplary life. I think we can agree on that. I think of the Bible stories as metaphors. I do not take them literally. I never have, even as a child."

Nabil pulled in front of Holy Name Cathedral, and I paid him. As I opened the door, he said, "Say a prayer for me, if you would."

I smiled and nodded. "I will."

I told my anesthesia group that I wanted back into the partnership track, to go back to working full time, taking trauma calls, and working at the hospital, or else I would find a job elsewhere. They told me that I could start taking call April 1 and would become a full partner in a year.

I made plans to travel, to visit old friends. I was done trying to make new friends. I gave up trying to date. I quit Match.com and ordered expanded cable with Turner Classic Movies and Sundance and Court TV instead.

I became comfortable staying home on Saturday nights by myself. I started working more, spending more time with Mom, reading more about the economy and business, and gradually I started to feel better.

On April 1, 2007, after nine years away, I took my first twenty-four-hour trauma call. I survived. So did the patients.

I felt the stress acutely. After working at an outpatient surgical center for four years, going back to the hospital was hard work, much harder than I'd been used to. The patients were sicker, the cases were bigger, the calls were . . . well, they were trauma calls. There's nothing to compare them to. Twenty-four hours of pure hell. We should get a merit badge just for surviving each and every one.

We see everything at the hospital, except for burns. Though it isn't a public hospital, like Cook County or Bellevue, with the weird inner-city shit that they get, we get a wider variety of industrial trauma, like injuries involving forklifts and punch presses. And we've begun to see more gang-related injuries being transferred in from the outlying suburbs. Our catchment area is huge, and it includes the airport.

I found that I brought something new to my group. I always liked the work. I liked the patients. I liked the nurses. I liked most of the surgeons. I felt welcomed back into the fold by nearly all. But now I had something more to offer, having been a patient myself; I had a sensitivity I hadn't had before.

Gradually I started to feel human again. Useful. Necessary. My work meant something. It gave me a frame of reference. It took time, but I was getting my skills back—doing trauma cases and big abdominal procedures requires a different skill set than doing tonsillectomies. I started feeling like a real doctor again. I gradually got used to the longer hours, the twenty-four-hour calls, the twelve-hour days. I was tired, but it felt like a good kind of tired. I had a way to define myself once again. The veil of depression slowly lifted, but not because of some sort of religious conversion.

I found out that I wasn't really a Catholic. If anything, I was a humanist who believed in God. I didn't believe in organized religion. I liked hearing that one priest speak. His kindness was not particularly Catholic or Christian. It was humane. He was the voice of compassion. I still enjoy his sermons.

My time became more structured, out of necessity, as I worked longer hours. Mom turned ninety early in the year and began requiring more and more attention. Each Saturday, after an aerobics class, I would take lunch to her condo. We shared a salad and a cookie, and then we would often go for a drive or out to shop. Sometimes we had our nails painted or drove through the Arboretum with Frank Sinatra playing on my iPod. Some days she didn't feel well enough to go outdoors, or didn't like the look of the weather, so we watched TV together. Then I rushed home to take care of Olga, who was still suffering not only from stress-induced colitis but from arthritis and old age.

Sundays I slept in, paid the bills, and did laundry. Occasionally I visited with friends. And then with friends of friends.

Responsibilities accumulated, friendships multiplied; I got busier and busier. The lack of a relationship in my life seemed almost unnoticeable. If I had enough to do, my life might pass for a life.

After four or five months, several friends offered to fix me up. I hesitated. I didn't feel ready. Then a friend at the health club told me about a dating service she'd used to meet her boyfriend. She said you go through an interview process, and the organization sets you up with age-appropriate men, typically one a month for a year, unless you want to stop or slow down. You meet the man for lunch or a drink, and the two of you take it from there. It's not cheap, but, she said, when people have to shell out money and go through an interview, they are more likely to be serious about actually wanting a relationship, about being ready for one. Another friend had a friend who also joined this organization and reported good results. My sister Bonnie had decided to try a similar group in the suburbs. Cautious but interested, I thought one date a month sounded like something I could manage. I agreed to let the friends fix me up.

I had lunch with a friend of a friend, and though he was a nice man, he had just retired. He wanted to travel. We were at completely different points in our lives and did not have much in common.

Soon afterward another friend fixed me up. Walter was a podiatrist, and had his own messy divorce recently behind him. We had zero chemistry and few common interests, except that we were both battle-scarred veterans of the same war. That seemed like enough, so we had dinner now and again. Walter talked enough for both of us, and when he called on the phone, I sometimes read the entire newspaper while I listened. This did not bother me, or seem to bother him. So every few weeks we met for dinner, or hit golf balls, or took a walk in the park.

After some deliberation, I decided to join Dating Alliance. I had not dated much as a kid, before I married. I needed to figure out what I wanted in a man. During all my dating experiences on Match.com, I'd wanted everyone to like me, and as a result, I had not learned much about men. I realized it was time for me to be a window shopper and find out what I wanted.

Contrary to the sales pitch of one date per month, the calls came once a week or more often. The women who worked in the Dating Alliance office were pushy and relentless about scheduling "dates" or "drinks" with the men they had arranged for me to meet.

I met number one, a bald divorced man who looked like Linus with a sunburn, for a quick drink. He had a sense of humor, so I agreed to have dinner with him a few days later. We met at my building, and as we waited for the traffic to clear and cross the street to his car, I looked both ways, as had become my habit. I looked away from number one, and then back toward him, to the right and then to the left, but as I turned my head back to the left, it (my head) was suddenly impaled on his tongue, which protruded from his head like a deranged crossing guard. Perhaps he thought this passed for a kiss. His tongue reminded me of a garden slug touched by rigor mortis. I said to number one, "I forgot some-thing. I've gotta go."

I turned around, and went back into my building.

Number two. Monosyllabic. 'Nuff said.

Number three turned out to be a physician and a golfing friend of my ex-brother-in-law. He talked a lot about declining reimburse-ments, the cost of college tuition, and his own plans to get braces in the near future. Number three then explained that he planned to call my ex-brother-in-law immediately to tell him of our meeting. I smiled and said, "Good-bye."

Number four was in real estate. He owned commercial proper-ties, which he then rented out to large successful franchises. He rubbed his hands together as he spoke of collecting his rents. He talked gleefully about the great deal he'd gotten on a luxury condo when some hapless couple had divorced mid-remodel, and he'd been the lucky profiteer. He even had heated towel bars, he bragged. When the bill came, I glanced at it lying between us. Here's a test, I thought to myself.

"Why don't we just split it?" I asked.

"That's fine," he said, failing the test concisely, "though your wine was two dollars more than my beer."

Chapter Sixteen

I CALLED THE women at Dating Alliance and told someone named Jane that I was frankly horrified by what they were sending me. Cheap cavemen without social skills were single for obvious anthropomorphic reasons. I needed a break, I said. A month off.

"Just one more. We have someone who's very interested in meeting you. Surely you can handle just one more date!"

Ugh, I thought. "Fine."

Charles was the fifth man I met through Dating Alliance. I gave in because they nagged me and I'd paid for it. Our first date coincided with the first day of the Neiman Marcus Last Call presale, sometime in mid-June, and I'd gone downtown to shop before meeting him at a restaurant in the Loop. I am clear on my priorities.

I felt unaccountably nervous—doubtful that I'd like him, afraid that I would. I had the cabdriver drop me three blocks from the restaurant so that I could walk off some of the anxiety. I'd met so many weird men by that point, I could not help but be jittery. Creeps and assholes predominated in the dating world, at least in my age range. I'd gotten better at recognizing them straight off, but as skills went, it still didn't rank in my top ten. Walter the podiatrist had *seemed* nice. But having good manners, I'd come to realize, was not the same as being a good person.

Anyway, I wasn't looking for anything serious. I just wanted to window-shop.

The major reservation in Charles's case—and there is always a reservation—was that he was sixty, Jane had told me. And as I told her, that's too old for me. Before she registered my complaint, she went on. He was originally from the Netherlands and owned his own manufacturing company, something in the airline industry. A very intelligent man, he spoke several languages. He was interested in travel, hiking, heli-skiing, and bike riding. I rarely listened to these synopses—I found them essentially meaningless, virtually interchangeable. Didn't they all ski? Didn't they all like live music? The girls at Dating Alliance put such a positive spin on everything and everyone that the only thing they didn't spin was age and height. I sometimes wondered what they said about me.

"It's one date," Jane said. "Surely you can handle just one date. If you don't like him—no big deal."

She made a reasonable argument. I hated that. Alex would be sixty now, wouldn't he? Fine. I reminded myself, I'd paid for this. On the other hand, I suspected that only real losers needed to use a dating service. What did this say about me?

So I arrived at the restaurant in the Loop at seven P.M. on a Thursday night in June, and Charles sat at the bar. He was tall, maybe six foot five, fit and trim, bald, with a skinny white handlebar mustache, and he looked every day of sixty. I thought, perhaps, he was older. Maybe sixty-eight or seventy. But they check the driver's licenses. Can you somehow lie?

Unlike the four previous dates I'd been with, Charles didn't want to sit at the bar and chat. He said he hadn't eaten. He asked if I would join him for dinner and told me that he would be happy to pay. We were shown to a table.

I did not find him attractive; I just found the mustache arresting, somewhat silly. I couldn't see past it. I kept thinking of Salvador Dalí. I tried to remember whether Dalí had hair. I thought he had hair. And wasn't his mustache black? Possibly dyed? Charles wore jeans that were dry-cleaned, and a crisply starched, white shirt with a little orange insignia embroidered on it. Mostly he just seemed old.

I'd dated someone his age before, which is to say, ten years older than me. And while Alex seemed older, he hadn't seemed this old. This man seemed ancient. This man seemed like my dad's age.

"I told the women at Dating Alliance my concern about dating someone with kids. But they assured me your kids are older. What do they do?"

I told him about Bea, working for a not-for-profit in the mental health sector.

"Does she live with you?"

"No," I said. "She moved out last fall into her own apartment. And my other daughter is in college in New York City. She has a couple of years to go. Do you have any kids?"

He launched into a description of his last marriage—*His last marriage?* I thought, *How many had there been?*—which had lasted ten years, and had ended essentially because he did not want children. He felt he was too old.

I'll say.

"Why don't you want to date anyone with kids?" I asked.

"Because they always come first," he said. Ah, I thought. Gita, my ex-therapist, would love this guy. He told me exactly who he was in the first five minutes. And then our menus arrived.

We talked about our dating experiences—he'd joined other services geared toward people with money, and I talked generically about my experiences with Match.com. He said he'd been on three previous dates through Dating Alliance, but the women were old and matronly. A theme kept coming up, I noticed, that he liked younger women. I asked him point-blank, what was wrong with women his age? Nothing, he said. Some of his best friends had been married to the same women for forty years.

"What about your work?" he asked me. "Are your hours predictable?"

"No," I answered. "Not particularly." I didn't sugarcoat it. "I work long, irregular hours, I take call, I work nights and weekends, and I often have no idea when I'm coming home until I walk out the door of the hospital."

"Do you think you'll be scaling back in the near future?"

"No," I answered. "I recently ramped up." He looked unhappy. I almost felt sorry for him. I could tell he very much wanted to fit me—a square peg—into the round hole that was the opening he'd made for a woman in his life. He didn't even know me, and he hadn't made any effort to know me, but he was already determining my suitability. And I wasn't doing anything to help him. Poor him. But since he was paying for dinner, I decided to be charitable. "Tell me about your work. I understand you're in manufacturing. I know a little about that—my family was in manufacturing."

He went into a description of his business, the difficulties particular to the airline industry, new advances in techniques, the logistical problems with outsourcing heavy materials and machinery. He talked about a new project he'd undertaken, an interesting venture with a brand-new technology that held great promise, and had a positive environmental impact, of which he was particularly proud. The more he talked, the more animated he became, and I began to see his passion for his work, which was not unappealing. The person who initially sat at the table and tried to spell out his requirements for a mail-order bride did not appeal to me at all. But this man, the man describing the culmination of his life's work, if not appealing, at least seemed worth knowing.

"For the last few years, I've commuted to my place in Palm Springs from October until April. I don't suppose you'd be able to do something like that. What are licensing requirements like in California, do you know?"

The guy had chutzpah, I'd give him that. "I have no idea," I answered. "But I don't know of any practices that allow their docs to come and go that way." I leaned forward and said, "Look. I've dated wealthy guys before, and it's always the same. They want you to drop your life and get on board theirs. Well, I'm not interested in that. I have a life, thank you very much. It's not all about money for me. I have a full, rich life, a meaningful, satisfying career, family here in Chicago, two beautiful daughters, lots of friends, and I don't need anybody or anything. So when I pick somebody I want to be with, it will be because I choose to be with him." I leaned back in my chair and figured that was that. He could pick up the check, and I would never see him again.

"Do you want coffee?" he asked.

"No thanks."

"Let's have two desserts."

"I don't want dessert."

"If you don't pick one, I'll pick them both."

"Fine."

As we left the restaurant, I headed across the street to grab a cab going north. A homeless man soundlessly walked up to Charles, who took out his wallet and handed him some money. I heard him murmur, "You're not going to drink all this, are you?"

"No, sir. I'm not."

"Can I call you?" Charles asked me.

I hesitated. He was too old for me. I wasn't attracted to him. He was controlling, probably narcissistic, one more of the same old same old; I'd been through it all before and hadn't I learned my lesson? Then again I just wanted to date. Casually. After all I'd been through, I wanted to just go out, meet people, and have some fun. I wanted a whole lot of Nothing Serious. So I thought a moment and then said okay. Mostly because of the homeless guy and because I just wanted to date and not everyone is going to be perfect when you just want to date and what's the big deal, right? And because old habits—like accommodating people who want something from you—die hard.

Charles waited two days to call me. I worked nonstop in between. And when he called, he asked if I would join him on a bike ride. He was building a new garage, and wanted to know what I thought about various brick colors and patterns. There were several he wanted to show me. Afterward we would have dinner. It was a fairly unique proposal, though ultimately negated by rain, and we ended up driving past his favorite brick examples in his car. Then he drove me past his home, to show me the original brick. After the tour, he asked if I had a preference for restaurants, and when I said no, he took me to a crowded, popular spot in the Near North area—his favorite restaurant—where it turned out he was well known. We were immediately shown to a table.

I thought his eating habits seemed odd—he liked everything very well done, including his vegetables. But we talked easily, and he asked about my family, my sisters, and my parents. He asked about my hobbies and wanted to know about my own remodeling projects and where I'd lived during my marriage.

"I think we should go slow, Margaret," he said to me. "Get to be friends first. You know? Not rush into anything. Sex, I mean."

That struck me as a weird statement, and I didn't respond, except with a generic *hmm* and a frown. I had not thought about having sex with him ever, but I'd learned that men are usually a step or two or ten ahead of women in this regard, or at least ahead of me. I didn't think I wanted to go out on another date with him, and he was probably picturing me naked. This is, in essence, the difference between the sexes, is it not?

He drove me home, and when we pulled in front of my building, he kissed me. The quick roughness of it startled me. I was uncomfortable, in an awkward position. And then he let me go.

I heard from him the next day.

He asked me out for that Friday night. I told him I didn't know how late I would be working. That was fine, he said. I could call him on my way home.

I worked with a surgeon named Fredo all day long on Friday. He is a busy general surgeon and a great guy who loves to tell jokes in the operating room. Because I have worked with him forever and we know each other well, I told him I had a date, so of course he wanted all the details. When I think of something soothing, like a lullaby or a John Lennon song, I also imagine a dirty joke whispered across the ether screen by Fredo.

Anyway, Fredo worked hard and fast to get me home by eight P.M.

so that I could have my date that night, though he was more excited about it than I was. I called Charles from the car, and he met
me at my building. He'd ridden his bike and brought me a couple
of books he thought I might enjoy reading. He stored his bike in
the back hallway, and we walked to the sushi place down the block
for dinner. It was a nice enough dinner, but I was exhausted. Conversation felt like work, and I'd already spent twelve hours in the
operating room. I don't remember what we ate or talked about.
After dinner we walked back to my condo. I had to take Olga for a
walk. Charles came with me, talking about his own pet, a Burmese
cat. And then we came back to the condo.

We were discussing the upcoming election, standing in the
kitchen, and then we wandered into the family room. He asked
me how I felt about Hillary Clinton. We both sat on the sectional
sofa, a few feet apart, facing each other.

"I like her views on health care," I said. "Forty-seven million
uninsured Americans is deplorable, it's obscene. All Americans
need to have health insurance."

"That's an unusual view for a physician."

"Maybe," I said. "Though I think many physicians believe there
needs to be better access to health care. Not everyone believes that
universal health insurance is the way to go. We recognize the ineq-
uity in the system, come smack up against it every day, and believe
there has to be a better way. We're just as affected by the insurance
companies as regular people are." I thought of my own inability
to get health insurance, of the aneurysm that would haunt me
indefinitely.

Suddenly his arm shot out behind me, and he grabbed my shoulder. I had my legs twisted up underneath me, leaning away from
him, and he pulled me off balance. He yanked me toward him, put

his mouth on mine, and kissed me, roughly, holding my neck tightly, sticking his tongue in my mouth. I pushed against his chest. We were on two different pieces of the sectional, and as he pulled at me, they started to separate. I had the thought—I couldn't say anything, his tongue stuffed in my mouth—health care turns you on? This all seemed absurd, apropos of nothing, and because of that I assumed he would stop. I assumed the best. I always assumed the best of people. Then he stuck one hand down my shirt and another hand inside my pants, pulling them down. My back was against the back of the sofa, but my hip was in the space between the two parts.

"Wait!" I said, when he lifted his mouth. I thought he was kidding, it seemed so ridiculous. He was joking, right? "What's going on here?" There'd been no preamble, no buildup. He was mauling me. He stuck his finger inside me.

"Oh, baby. You make my penis so hard."

"*What?* Hold on a second. This is crazy." He grabbed my hand and pushed it against his pants. He was, indeed, hard. When did that happen?

"I want you, Margaret."

"I don't know you well enough. No! Are you turned on by Hillary Clinton?" I kept thinking that he was kidding. This was all crazy, a joke. It was as if someone had flipped a switch, and he went from being a normal person to being a sex maniac in an instant.

"You want me to stop?" he asked.

"Yes!" I said. "Yes! I want you to stop!"

Then he turned almost tender and slowed. I turned my head. I wanted to get a breath that didn't include him, didn't include his scent, but for that moment, I must have relaxed, and the tension must have lessened imperceptibly. It was enough. He flipped on top of me and yanked my pants down. As he did that, the two pieces of furniture that made up my sofa widened further. My bare bottom hung suspended between them.

I said again, "I don't know you well enough. Stop!" I thought, He knows I want him to stop. So he'll do the right thing. He will stop.

Then he opened his pants and took out his penis.

"See how hard you make me?"

I could not see him, his head was right next to mine. He was huge and heavy. Gradually, I lost the sense of being in my own body, and then I was above it, watching it all happen from the corner ceiling of my family room. I thought about screaming, but it was as if the thought had occurred to someone else. It was summertime, and my cross-the-hall neighbor was living in Michigan. Had I mentioned that to him? Probably I had. No, I remembered, he'd asked, specifically. This was an old building, well insulated. I thought of the times I'd blasted rock and roll. No one ever complained. And now, if I were to scream, would anyone hear me? Unlikely. I never heard anyone. I thought if I fought him, he might get more excited, and he might hurt me more. Something about him wasn't right, really not right. I wasn't afraid for myself, exactly, I couldn't acknowledge any fear, that seemed worse, but it was as though someone else lay there, with her bare butt hanging ridiculously suspended a foot over the floor as this old man tried to shove his penis inside her. I floated above it all, watching, waiting for sanity to return.

I said, enunciating clearly, as my mother had taught me to do, as if to a child, "Charles, if you do this, I will never see you again. Do you understand that? Is that what you want?"

"No," he said. He shoved himself inside me and pounded away.

I wonder now at the physical impossibility of it all—how he managed intercourse with me suspended between two pieces of furniture. I supposed he must have held my hips up somehow, though I don't actually remember. I know he came quickly, and I vaguely remember him grunting. When it was over, I pushed at him, saying, "I hope you don't have any diseases."

"I hope you don't either," he said, as if this had been a mutual endeavor, a mutual decision to forgo all discussion of birth control, sexual histories, and so on and so forth, a mutual decision to take this relationship to the next level. As if we had cared about each other, or as if he had cared about what I thought or felt or wanted. But there had been nothing mutual about it. There had been no mutuality in his kisses, no reciprocity in his touch. I thought his comment sounded exactly like something my ex-husband would have said. He just—took. I hated all men in that moment.

He sat up, and I quickly crawled off what was left of the sofa, taking my clothing with me and ran down the hall to my bathroom. I sat on the toilet and squeezed my pelvic muscles with all my might—forcing whatever bodily fluids of his might still remain inside me out. I'd read an article once about Polynesian women without birth control who did Kegel exercises to expel semen. Not that I needed to worry about birth control, but he hadn't used a condom. I wasn't thinking clearly. I grabbed a washcloth and soap and cleaned myself and brushed my hair and pulled it tight into a bun. I scrubbed my face. After standing before the mirror for a few moments, without seeing myself, I went back into the family room. He sat there casually, on the sofa, fully dressed. He'd pushed the two parts back together. He smiled at me, a smug ugly smile. He looked like he was a hundred years old. In that moment he was not Charles but Stig too and Alex and Max and Mitchell. He was every man who had ever used me, mistreated me, not come through for me when I needed him. He was every man who had ever taken what he'd wanted, simply, and without regard for a woman, any woman. I hated them all. I hated him, but he was all of them wrapped up in one body, one ugly, ugly body.

I sat across from him, on the coffee table, and wrapped my arms about my knees. I didn't smile back. I felt suffused with an inexplicable calm, as if I were going into battle. After a moment I started to talk. I told him a story, a parable I suppose you could call it. I didn't know why then, or where it came from, but I told him the story of my divorce.

I told him about going to trial, about testifying, about being on the witness stand for three days. I told him the whole thing, every ugly detail. I told him that I'd done a lot of things in my life, trauma cases, open heart surgery; that I'd had patients, including children, die on the operating table, on my watch; that I'd given my own father morphine to help him as he lay dying, then delivered the eulogy at his funeral Mass; but that nothing was as difficult as sitting in that courtroom. I told him how, when it was all over, Stig asked if we could please be friendly, have dinner now and again, because divorce was just an extreme sport, wasn't it? Everybody acted that way—get as much as you can.

I took a deep breath and said, "I told him *no*. He had gone too far—he had lost me for good. He'd lost my friendship. From then on he could contact me through my attorney. No writing, calling, or e-mailing. As far as I was concerned, he was dead."

I wasn't certain why, at the time, I told Charles this story; nor did it make any sense to me for a long time afterward.

He asked, "Did you ever cheat on him?"

"No," I answered. And with that I smiled, but my stomach turned.

I told Charles to go home. As he passed my golf clubs in the hall, he made a gesture toward them. "You know, you might have to get rid of these," he said. I supposed that meant Charles envisioned a future with me. Charles didn't golf.

I opened the door, he walked out, and I quickly locked it behind him. I never used to lock my doors. But I guess I'd never had evil in my home before.

I went to a wedding the next night, with Walter the podiatrist as my escort. It was, I think, our fifth date. I know that before the wedding I visited my mom, had my nails done, and a pedicure, and I bought a wedding present. I guess I bought some shoes—I have the receipt, but no clear recollection of any of it. I remember Walter picking me up, and getting into his car. I remember the drive to the Chicago Yacht Club. I did not know the bride and groom. The groom's father and stepmother were my friends.

At the end of the evening, Walter and I sat outside and watched the fireworks from Navy Pier. He said to me, "You seem very pensive tonight."

I wrapped myself tight in a shawl. I nodded and shivered. But I did not feel pensive. I felt the numbness of shock.

The next morning, a Sunday, I woke up, made coffee, and sat down to read the paper. The phone rang. It was my daughter Ruthann, who was in summer school in New York.

"How were your dates, Mommy?" she asked.

I burst into tears.

I told her I did not want to see Charles again. That was all I knew at the time. I was horrified by what had happened and somehow felt that I could have controlled it, could have prevented it. He had called that morning, and seeing his number on the caller ID, I hadn't picked up. Seeing the number terrified me. I did not want to speak to him or see him. I felt revulsion at what had happened, at what we had done. I did not want to have sex with him, and I had told him that. I did not utter the word *rape*—I did not even think it. I called and left a message for my therapist. It would be two days before I said the word—but somehow Ruthann understood. As I told her my confused, disjointed account of date rape that I could not yet identify as such, my twenty-one-year-old daughter understood exactly what had happened. Her level of sensitivity amazed me and saddened me. Her ability to vocalize the feelings I was feeling, to help me take the steps I needed to take, would help me start to talk about it. And when I eventually started to talk about it, the ubiquity of the experience, among women, old and young, among gay men, shocked me beyond belief.

Chapter Seventeen

RAPE CAN MAKE a person catatonic. It did that to me, initially. Days passed. Weeks. I barely blinked. I lay in bed without sleeping. I worked, I biked, and I slept, sort of. I repressed every thought, every feeling. I wore headphones while walking Olga, while riding my bike, while walking to the pharmacy or the coffee shop. I had music playing everywhere at all times, at home and in the car, loud enough so that I could not think even if I wanted to. Or else I hid out at the hospital. Working long hours, I felt safest there. I did not want to socialize or be with friends, particularly. I just wanted to work, be responsible for others. It kept my mind off myself, off how I felt, or rather it kept me from feeling. I wanted to be useful to the point of exhaustion, so I could not feel anything else. I wanted to help other people, because that was what I was trained to do. That's my default setting. And when I could not do that, I rode my bike.

Interestingly, it was one of my partners, Sam, who said to me, "Overton, what's the matter with you?"

"You don't want to know," I said. In case it isn't clear by now, I do not claim adeptness at small talk; nor do I lie well. We sat together eating lunch in the Anesthesia Library. It was an early afternoon in mid-July.

"Actually, I do. You're not yourself. You haven't been for a couple of weeks. What's going on?"

My eyes watered. "I don't want to talk about it."

"Okay, but maybe you'd better talk about it," he said. The group had hired Sam to replace Paul when he died. He has movie star looks and a perpetual tan.

"Are you sure you want to know?"

"Yes."

"I was raped."

"Oh, Margaret," he said, "I'm so sorry."

"Me too."

"Did he hurt you?"

I smiled. "That's an interesting question."

"Of course he hurt you. But I mean physically."

"No," I said. "Not really."

"How do you feel?" he asked.

"I feel terrible. But I don't want to talk about it."

Gradually, I told people. First Hayley and Kate, then my sisters. It took me a long time to tell Bea. And when I did, I blamed myself because I'd trusted a stranger. Isn't that what we teach our children never to do? I'd assumed the best of someone without even knowing him. I was naïve, but it seemed more complicated than that. I took things at face value. I did not look for evil, I believed what people told me, I believed the best not just of him but of everyone I knew. I'd done it my whole life. There were all sorts of red flags I'd ignored.

Charles had told me he had several different cars, so each time I went outside, I was paranoid that he would follow me.

I did not answer his phone calls. He called and left messages for a week or so, then stopped.

He had left books at my condo for me to read. I sent them back to him with a terse note. "Leave me alone."

My sister Beth's husband Andrew called one Sunday morning. Andrew is in his sixties, a gentle giant. "Why don't you go to the police, Margaret?"

"I can't," I said. "I can't go through that."

Several men—Andrew, Sam, my friend Ben—asked me why I hadn't reported the rape. Women rarely asked that question.

While I was in medical school, I did rape victim counseling, so I knew the rules. You cannot wash anything off. You have to go to the emergency room or to the police for evidence collection. But not washing, and taking your unwashed, violated self to strangers for examination, goes against your instincts, which are to wash everything away, to scrub the filth off of you, immediately.

And having recently experienced the United States judicial system, I was not willing to experience it again. I knew he would have higher-priced lawyers than I would, that the system might have been designed with me in mind but had been implemented for hundreds of years with him in mind, and the protection of his legal rights would be of paramount importance. Men rape women all the time. But . . . I had let him in my home. Therefore I tacitly approved of anything he might want to do to me. Try to prove otherwise. That's how they get away with it. I would not be the person to change that. Maybe at some other time, at some other age—but the fight had left me.

Gradually, as I spoke to friends and family, the shock gave way to rage. He was not Charles; he was every man. Charles did what Charles had been doing to women his entire life. He had the mind of a criminal. I just happened to cross his path. He became an abstraction to me. I hated not just him but every narcissistic monster I'd ever known. And hadn't I only known such men? Didn't the world teem with them? Banks, politics, Wall Street, maybe even parts of medicine—these fields ran on the blood of men devoted to their own self-interest. If they weren't raping women, they were raping the less advantaged, the economy, the future, the environment. Self-interest for today, fuck everybody else and their tomorrows. What was it about me that had been drawn to these men repeatedly? They crawled all over our backs to get ahead, wreaking havoc, taking taking taking. I'd been on this merry-go-round ever since I could remember. I did not have a clue how to exit.

I could not manage my rage, and that's what I tried to do. Manage it. So I read everything I could—from articles about personality disorders to evolutionary psychological theory of rape to articles about so-called ethnic cleansing in war-torn areas throughout history. I became obsessed with psychopathology, learned about functional MRIs and who was studying criminal behavior where and why and how. I read about perverts and serial killers, and I found poems about narcissism by authors as diverse as Tony Hoagland to Alan Dugan. Intellectualization of the act, seeing it in the broader, anthropological view, made it easier for me to get to sleep at night. This rape occurred in my new condo—my newly renovated condo—the first home I'd ever created for my daughters and myself. Everything about this new place had been independent of Stig, from the paintings on the walls to my grandmother's piano on which I'd learned to play from the time I was four. Charles had defiled my home as well as me. I could not bear it.

I called the woman in charge of Dating Alliance. I told her what had happened. She sent me a check for the remainder of my unused money. I feel certain she discussed the situation with her attorney. I would have done the same in her situation.

Like most women, I'd feared rape in the abstract. Now I know why. It stays with you—the violence and the fear and the intimidation—it stays with you, in small and large ways, and it screws up your life and your relationships for years. But while it is a sexual act, it is only marginally about sex. It is an assertion of power, an act of intimidation. It is a violent crime. I had read about this before, but now I had experienced it personally.

And yet because of its sexual nature, because of the nature of intimacy, rape results in a cross-contamination of violence and sex. Feminist Carol Hanisch said, "The personal is the political." I never really understood that statement before then. Now I understand it too well, in a way I wish I didn't.

You can have sex again, but to have a normal relationship again, to look at a man, to trust again, that's where the disconnect occurs. Trust—that's the trickiest issue. Trust becomes as fragile as spun sugar, easily broken, the first thing to be sacrificed. Trust is fucking evanescent. I knew who I could trust—myself, my daughters, my sisters, my friends. These were a lot of women, but some men too, and a lot of dead people. Why on earth would I ever bother trusting anyone new again?

If you think that's any different for a young girl, or a poor girl, or a married woman, or someone with a supportive, loving mate, I would beg to differ.

At any moment, your life can change. I could not forget it. Not even for a second. Life kept teaching me the same goddamn lesson, over and over.

After the rape, the only relief I found was in riding my bike, the constant motion of it. I rode every day I could—twenty-five miles along the lakefront, in Michigan on day trips, along the Green Bay Trail with Hayley, and in the suburbs when I visited my mom. I wore headphones to not think and rode and rode and rode.

Gita, my therapist, told me time and again, "Margaret, do things that make you feel better. Whatever they may be."

I went to a spa for a few days. I went to exercise classes, had massages, and floated in the pool in the afternoons. I studied the insects and let the sun bake me.

I found old interviews with Carl Jung on YouTube and watched them repeatedly. It made me feel better to hear him speak, to see him in his home office on Lake Zurich, to hear his views on death and the psyche. He said, "We are the origin of all common evil."

Eventually I made tentative plans. I hadn't been able to think further than a day or two ahead after the aneurysm. I think that's pretty common after a near-death experience. But now I tried to envision a future alone, finally, and while I didn't exactly welcome it, I didn't seem to have much choice. I had bad judgment about men, but fairly good judgment about nearly everything else. How had that happened? I trusted the wrong men, repeatedly. Friends told me I had bad luck, but I knew it was more than that. There was something about me, something that attracted bad people. I would be turning fifty in the spring. I'd never been one to dread birthdays before, but something about turning fifty felt awful. Did anything good happen after fifty? Decay, decrepitude, dementia—I only knew I did not want to live in a place like my mother lived. I had the idea of creating my own retirement community somewhere, with people I liked. Maybe I'd buy some property. I envisioned a series of cottages around a centralized lodge. Of course, I wasn't there yet, but I should start looking. In the meantime, deal with fifty first. The best way to approach it was to travel nonstop, party nonstop, visit friends, take a bike trip, go everywhere, do everything, try and not sit still for even one freaking minute. Maybe I'd go visit Lake Zurich someday, Jung's home. I had a week of vacation in October and decided to take a bike trip. I contacted an active-travel company and spoke to a sales associate.

"There's a singles and solos trip to Napa Valley that has space and coincides with your dates. How does that sound?"

Jung was dead; wine sounded like a reasonable substitute. Napa wasn't Zurich, but I could afford it.

I cycled hundreds of miles in preparation for the trip—I was in training, not just escaping from my life. The summer was very hot, and I rode some days along the lakefront when it was ninety-three or ninety-five degrees. I developed a biker's tan. Very gradually it occurred to me that I knew how to take care of other people, how to listen, how to be supportive, how to be empathic—to my mom, to my kids, to my patients, to my friends and coworkers when they needed me, to friends who were divorcing, to friends who'd suffered loss, to friends with illness—but I had no clue how to take care of myself. I knew that exercise was good. And listening to music was good. But I also knew they constituted a distraction. For the time being, distraction would have to suffice. I couldn't manage anything more. It was all I knew about taking care of Margaret.

Shortly after Labor Day, Bea and I spent a weekend in New York City with Ruthann. We wandered through MoMA and the

Guggenheim and Central Park, sat in bars on the Lower East Side and drank wine together. My bland fragility scared the girls, made them squabble and pick on each other. Stig had remarried that summer, then told them long after the fact. Gradually I realized they were struggling and I was part of the problem. My daughters wanted me to be the mother I'd been years before, the role model mother. They wanted her back. I wanted her back. A friend reminded me of a Buddhist saying: *Practice precedes insight.* Biking alone for hours wearing headphones would not cure me of my trauma. I didn't know what would, exactly, but perhaps if I practiced acting like a healthy person, I might eventually become one.

Chapter Eighteen

IT'S A TYPICAL Friday in early fall. I work at the hospital until three P.M., then drive to my mom's condo at the retirement community. I organize her pills for the week while we watch *Divorce Court* with Judge Lynn Toler and laugh until Mom's neighbor stops by to pick her up for dinner. I do not join them in the dining room, claiming I have other plans, but I don't. I simply cannot stand to eat there. The institutional food appeals only to those over eighty, scientifically proven to have no taste buds whatsoever, and I can't get used to eating dinner at five P.M.

I sit in traffic for an hour going into the city, then stop at a gourmet grocery store near Navy Pier to pick up something for dinner, along with a bottle of wine. I like this grocery store because it sells very few things you actually have to prepare for yourself. My gourmet cooking days seem like a distant memory. Between long hours at work, caring for my dog, visiting Mom, and riding my bike, cooking has become an activity that's lost appeal and/or relevance. Food is for sustenance; I survive on carry-out and delivery. I cook only for Olga, who has a delicate constitution and requires poached chicken and steamed rice with organic chicken broth twice a day, sometimes with a little pumpkin mixed in for fiber. Her third meal consists of canned prescription dog food, whereby she obtains her necessary vitamins and minerals. I have become *one of those dog people*.

The upscale grocery store, on a Friday evening, is mobbed with middle-aged city couples, whose casual hipness irritates from the moment I walk through the sliding door. I feel certain they've been placed there by God to highlight my loneliness and test my resolve. It's been a long day, a long week, and a really long life. I grab a mini-cart and stop to peruse the ready-made Caesar salads for $7.95, rummaging to the back of the cooler for one with an expiration date beyond a day or two. I take a bag of organic granola but bypass the meat department and head for the cheese-monger. We're old friends. He gives me a nod as I get into line.

"Would anyone like to try the Cashel Bleu?" he asks, as he cuts a chunk for the first customer in line. I've discovered the ease and practicality of a cheese-and-crackers dinner, with a small variety of fruit on the side, because fruit is almost like a vegetable, and when it accompanies the protein-rich cheese, the meal seems nearly healthful. Add a glass of wine, and you've covered your basic food groups. Sort of. I glance around at the others waiting.

Unfortunately, the line consists of two or three alarmingly handsome and fit gray-haired men with arms draped around fashionable, model-thin forty-year-old women dressed by Dries Van Noten and the like. My reflux starts to act up. Did I leave my Rolaids in the car? I feel a headache coming on. Maybe I'll skip the cheese today, just go home and get into bed, watch a week's worth of *The Daily Show* on the Internet. As I turn to move toward the Everything Already Prepared section, another twosome blocks the path of my cart. Mr. Dashing Art Director delicately places a dollop of Cashel

Bleu into his Gorgeous Matching Partner's mouth as she sighs and fakes a cheesy orgasm. They kiss. My eyes roll nearly into the back of my head. I've been to Connemara in Ireland, okay? I stayed at Cashel House with Stig years ago. While watching these artsy two swap spit, I suddenly recall an incident at that stunning manor house around foreign plumbing. I had turned on the tub water, which activated the unsecured handheld showerhead—a long, thick hoselike apparatus. With the water running, it behaved as a snake in the throes of a grand mal seizure, whipping a full nozzle of cold spray wildly throughout the charming bathroom, soaking old family portraits hanging on the walls, while I, starkers, shrieking and freezing, struggled to get control of the crazy, twisting, spewing thing. Who puts family portraits in the bathroom anyway? I head straight for the wine.

I've come to an important conclusion: I'm not like other people. I don't have something they have. I snatch two containers of organic yogurt and pull a U-turn around the imported EVOOs. Yet another adorable couple canoodles in the pasta aisle. I reach for a salami, think twice, and back up. I feel myself hyperventilating, but love is in the air, and I want to spit it out. By the time I arrive at the checkout lane, I've added a quart of Oberweis Vanilla Ice Cream and an extra bottle of Pinot Noir to the grocery cart, though I'm not sure why I bother with the other stuff. Screw the vegetables, if you call lettuce a vegetable, which I do. I really only want the ice cream and wine. I'm even tempted to skip my usual main course of peanut butter and jelly.

At the checkout line I get behind yet another nauseatingly perfect couple in this Noah's ark of torment, in this world where true singles are outsiders, losers, and loners. Come to think of it, all my gay friends are couples too. If this grocery store were Noah's ark,

I'd drown. I cannot get out of here fast enough. I take a deep cleansing breath. Drudge up some fucking inner peace, Margaret. I can do this. I can get through this checkout line without sticking a plastic fork in my eye. I glance up.

The man appears to be my age—blondish, fit, trim. Too handsome for his shirt, which looks fifties and dental. He casually bags their groceries. The woman has her back to me, but from behind I see mile-long legs in skin-tight jeans on top of tall wedgie sandals, a striped tube top, and long, artfully streaked hair. Did I mention skinny, skinny but perfectly buff arms? She's probably twelve, I think to myself, and attempt another cleansing breath. I glance around for the plastic forks, just to keep one handy.

And then she turns toward me and smiles. I may have gasped, audibly.

She has had, it's fair to say, or been the victim of, the worst plastic surgery I've ever seen. Ever. No kidding. I cannot stop staring. I have no idea how old she is. She might be thirty, she might be seventy. It's hard to tell. She might have once been attractive. But now she is a monster in a mask.

And yet the amazing thing is that she still gets the guy. Sure she has great fake boobs, but her face looks unevenly stretched, stitched, taut, fake—and creepy. There's a disconnect between her head and the rest of her body. Can she feel her face? Can she feel her own nipples?

There is some serious weirdness in this world. I wonder about it a lot.

Might I be alone because I won't have plastic surgery? Or am I alone because I don't want to be with someone who wants to be with a woman who will be surgically altered for his benefit? I could be wrong—maybe she did this because she wanted to undergo pain and suffering to look like a plastic imitation of a human. Am I alone because I think this way?

Or am I alone because I think?

Then again, what's the matter with being alone? I guess there are people who can do it, and there are people who cannot. It takes a long time to understand how much you're willing to give up in order to be part of a couple.

I study the woman in the tube top. I imagine various scenarios. Maybe she's eighty-five and having a fine old time with her fifty-year-old stud-muffin. Go for it, girlfriend! Perhaps she has a sterling personality inside that surgically altered head. I have platinum inside *my* head, but it did nothing for my looks. I cannot help but wonder, though, what is so terrible about aging? It happens to everyone. Some part of you will always give away your age; even your obvious addiction to plastic surgery announces to the world your discomfort with who or what you are.

And if you have it done, do it for yourself, and do your research. There are too many hacks out there.

Sam pops into my OR at work.

"Margaret, I gotta talk to you."

"What is it, Sam?"

"I, uh, my wife is filing for divorce."

"Oh, Sam, I'm so sorry." I mean it. I know what awaits him. *The horror.*

"I know, me too. I'm just devastated. Heartbroken. I feel as if I've been kicked in the teeth. I don't want it, I don't know why she wants it, but she seems convinced this is the only way. I can't talk her out of it. I suppose, in my usual guy fashion, it had been coming on for a while, and I didn't pay attention, so it seemed like it came out of nowhere, but to her, she'd been unhappy for a while, I guess. Anyway, I feel terrible. I've never been so down in my life."

"I'm really sorry. It's a hard thing to go through. If there's anything I can do—"

"Well, actually, I was thinking . . ."

Sam leans close so that he can speak quietly into my ear. We both wear paper masks and paper hats, green scrubs, blue paper gowns.

"I'm looking for a 'friends with benefits' type of situation, if you know what I mean. I have needs, and this has been rough on me."

I lean back and look him in the eye.

Are all men pigs? Are all men completely despicable, revolting, worthless pieces of shit? I think they may be genetically mutated porcine because, in my experience, the evidence grows more conclusive by the day. I actually like Sam. I think he's relatively nice, as far as men go. But my standards plummet with each and every man I get to know.

"Sam, there's a reason God gave you two hands. Use them."

His eyes crinkle up. "Margaret, look at these hands." He holds his palms out for me to see. "They've got calluses."

We laugh, but then I say to him, seriously, "You know, people going through a divorce need to be careful, because they can do a lot of collateral damage. You're a disaster right now. You are a walking disaster. You know it, and I know it. You think it's only in one small area of your life, but it's not. It spills over into every area, into every relationship, and it poisons everything. So I'll be your friend, because you need a friend a lot more than you need someone to sleep with." There should be a mentoring program for people going through divorce. I mean it, a national divorce hotline.

Sam and I are still good friends. He thinks I gave him good advice.

When he occasionally asks if I've changed my mind yet (oink, oink), I say, "The list of reasons I won't sleep with you is as long as my arm. Do you want to hear it?"

He shakes his head and answers, "No. No, I don't. You're right. I am a disaster."

Another friend, James, told me a story about a buddy of his who went through a divorce and all he could think about was getting laid. No introspection, no regrets. Just wanted to get laid. In general, this mind-set did not bode well for his next marriage, as far as I could tell. So he went to bars and went up to women and said, "Fuck-ee, fuck-ee?" He would do this, on average, several hundred times a night.

I asked if he was ever successful.

Yes, surprisingly. He is successful approximately one in several hundred times. He thinks this works better than drinks and dinner, or dinner and a movie—never a sure bet by any means, and the price is definitely right.

This technique was about quantity, clearly, and not about quality, not about "moving on."

Thomas is my handsome friend who also saved my life, neurosurgically speaking. We went to school together and have worked together forever, I knew his ex-wife, and my daughters babysat for his kids. We socialized when we were both married. When he is between girlfriends, we sometimes go out for dinner. One evening in the fall, we meet for a Thai dinner near the hospital. We know each other very well.

"I read something in the newspaper the other day that got me thinking," I tell him.

"What's that?"

As usual, Thomas has no money. He is a busy, successful neuro-surgeon, and I pay for dinner. This seems wrong, but I forgive him because he saved my life. I even love him for that.

"The article said that for most of the past hundred thousand years, the average life expectancy for humans was twenty-seven to thirty. By 1800, it had extended to forty-seven. It said that women, in the year 2005, could expect to live seven years longer than their mothers. My mother was eighty-eight in 2005. That would theo-retically, aside from the aneurysm and the fact that we have no idea what that will do to me personally, put my life expectancy at ninety-five."

Thomas looks at my uneaten pad thai with longing. "You going to eat that?"

"No, go ahead," I answer.

"So what's your point?" he asks.

"My point is not about life expectancy. My point is about mar-riage," I say.

"Okay. What about marriage?" Thomas and I have discussed both of our marriages and our divorces in detail. He left his wife for another woman, but that relationship has also ended.

"In the past hundred years, our life expectancy has doubled. Back in the 1800s, when we were at home on the farm, with a hus-band and a kid or two and a couple of cows and pigs and a goat, and nobody was educated, there was no television, and no telephone, or cars, or Internet, people were cut off from the outside world. Infi-delity didn't exist, as much, for lack of opportunity and probably out of exhaustion. Now, we're bombarded by sexual stimulation in the media, pornography is more accessible, expectations are com-pletely different, both partners work long hours outside the home, and there's a steady stream of readily available people to cheat with! So it's a different situation.

"And yet, nothing about marriage has changed, except how long we expect it to last. That's doubled. My parents argued constantly for fifty-seven years. So it isn't as though we were taught anything about how to stay married. Sure, they blathered on about compromise, and sacrifice, and give and take, and that once kids come along, everything changes totally. But in my family my dad did exactly what he wanted, and my mom compromised, and sacrificed, and made do. And behind his back she made a fist and ugly hand gestures. She didn't teach me anything about being married, except to suck it up and be miserable.

"So how do you learn? How do we teach our kids to choose mates? Especially if we don't know ourselves. We just watch people go blindly into it, often completely ill suited for each other, and then watch as they fail. Then we talk about the downfall of society based on the abysmal divorce statistics. Whereas, I think it's a miracle that anybody actually stays married for even twenty years. I think a twenty-year marriage should be considered a success. I guess what I'm getting at is that there should be something required in order to obtain that marriage license, something besides proof that you don't have syphilis. Do they still require that? And how old were you when you met your wife?"

"Fourteen. I married the only woman I ever slept with," Thomas says, looking glum.

"I was twenty-one. And an idiot."

"Margaret, you were never an idiot." Thomas smiles. He is a good, loyal friend. Little does he know.

"I don't think it's any wonder that people cheat," I say. "It's often a symptom and not the disease. I suppose, in some cases there are chronic philanderers who just shouldn't marry. Which isn't to say that I think it's okay. I think if you need to do it, you should do the right thing and tell your spouse. And separate. I think the bad part is the dishonesty. I'm just not sure marriage is relevant anymore. I wish there were some other way to legitimize and raise children."

Thomas looks thoughtful. "Marriage should be a contract that comes up for renewal every fifteen years, you know? Not automatic. You want to provide some stability for the kids but at the same time voluntarily renew. I know I got married too young. I never had a chance to sow my wild oats." He smiles.

I have a sense he is doing it now, but I don't say anything. "I didn't either," I say. "And when I finally did, it wasn't as much fun as I'd hoped."

We are all screwed up, all of us, men and women alike. Something about the idea of marriage or a relationship is so seductive, so compelling, that it sucks people in. Women are focused on the marriage itself, the money and security; men are obsessed with youth and trophy looks or just getting laid. Shallow people have it the best—they don't expect much, and they're not as disappointed. But if you want something more than that, good luck. The problem is that we all think marriage is something we should know how to do, and when we fail at it, we're flummoxed. It takes years to get over the damage that divorce inflicts. And just when we think we are on the road to recovery, we get thrown completely off course.

Chapter Nineteen

THE BUS BOUND for Napa Valley left from outside a hotel in San Francisco's Union Square district on a Sunday morning, in mid-October. I'd spent the night nearby in an old but refurbished hotel recommended by the travel company after arriving late in the evening. They'd instructed us to wear biking attire for the ride to Napa, as we'd set off as soon as we arrived, but I knew better. We would meet our guides, do introductions, eat lunch, get outfitted for our bikes, be given safety instructions, and have access to restrooms. I walked up to the group and saw women with their helmets on, men in brightly colored jerseys. I was in the right place.

Although I'd done these cycling vacations before, this trip marked my first time alone. I felt awkward and shy.

A younger woman, in her late thirties, thin and very fit, stuck out her hand. "Hi, I'm Micheline," she said.

"Margaret," I said. "It's nice to meet you."

A dark-haired man walked up to us, in biking gear and a jacket. "Henry," he said, "from New York," and held out his hand.

"Margaret," I repeated, and shook it. Micheline repeated her name for Henry.

This went on for ten minutes or so, while a small crowd gathered, making desultory conversation about previous cycling trips. A group of twelve eventually boarded the bus, planning to make a stop for another two bikers at another hotel. As I climbed onto the bus, Henry asked if he could sit with me. I glanced at him. About my age, or a few years older, Henry seemed nice enough. Not particularly handsome, certainly not ugly, just slightly eager.

"That's fine," I answered. "Whatever."

I sat in the seat behind the driver, next to the window. Henry asked me where I was from, was I married, did I have children. Had I been biking long, had I been to Napa before, had I biked with this travel company in the past. The questions went on and on, but the view as we crossed the bridges interested me more, and I stared out the window at the scenery. I didn't feel like making small talk. There were lots of women on this trip, not too many men, and I felt certain that Henry would move on. He seemed like an accomplished extrovert, whereas I was still actively cultivating inner peace. All in all, things had improved in that regard. I did not want a man to come along and interfere with the progress I'd made. The summer had taken a lot from me; I had energy for biking, but not much else. This was the road to recovery.

We arrived in Sonoma, ate lunch during which Henry sat beside me, and started biking from the Bouchaine Vineyards. The roads, that first day, were empty, the sky blue, the vineyards golden, and the group quickly spread itself out. I had no interest in hurrying, and I planned to bike alone, at my own pace, see the country, take pictures. I wasn't sure why I'd come on this trip—socializing with strangers seemed like the equivalent of a root canal. Why hadn't I gone to another spa, somewhere I could be alone, float in a pool, read, exercise when I felt like exercising? I'd signed up for the trip back in July, when I was in pure survival mode, and biking was the only activity I had to maintain sanity. So now here I was, surrounded by an odd assortment of people I couldn't relate to, wondering what the hell I was doing.

Henry cycled with me, or behind me, all day. He asked more questions. I answered, briefly, to be polite, and gradually the beautiful day and his genial company lifted my mood.

A few miles before reaching our hotel, Henry caught his tire on the edge of the road and fell off his bike. I stopped, dismounted, removed my helmet and gloves, and assessed the damage: doctor mode. His elbow was scraped and swollen, but his forearm was badly abraded and bleeding, as he'd fallen hard in some gravel. He'd injured his leg too, but that wound was superficial. I had first aid supplies in my bike bag, and gathered them together.

He held out his arm. I had antiseptic spray, some wipes, bandages. "This is going to hurt," I told him, and sprayed, cleaning his arm with the limited equipment I had available.

He didn't scream or flinch, but I wasn't really looking at his face. I put Band-Aids on his wounds, then helped him with his bike gloves.

That night the group met for a drink before dinner. Henry came to the circle we sat in, wearing a dress shirt with one sleeve open. He sat beside me.

"Can you button my cuff for me?" he asked. "I can't get it with this elbow."

I buttoned his cuff, and everyone in the group noticed. You don't need a doctor to button your shirt, I thought. After I buttoned his cuff, it occurred to me that an elbow injury should not prevent a person from being able to button his own shirt if he possessed any degree of dexterity. Boy, was I gullible.

I sat with a different group at dinner. I met Ken and Cindy and Jan and Julia and Arlene. Right after dinner I excused myself and went to bed.

The second day we rode from the town of Sonoma toward the coast, stopped at Matanzas for a wine tasting, and ended up at Bodega Bay. Once again, all day, Henry rode with me. He seemed an inexperienced rider and appeared to enjoy my leisurely pace. We stopped in St. Helena for more bandages and first aid supplies, and a few of us checked out the art galleries. Henry and I spoke easily; we told stories about our children, about ourselves, about friends. I think we were trying to understand why we were both alone and on vacation. He was still married, he told me, though he'd been separated, off and on, for quite a while.

I didn't ask exactly what that meant. But I registered the fact that Henry was a married man who'd signed up for the singles and solos bike trip. That felt a little off, but who was I to judge? My own divorce had taken three and a half years. I dated a lot during that time.

The scenery changed with each turn of a corner, as the sun moved across the sky, as the grapevines came and went. I stopped to take pictures of cows, and the vineyards where the leaves sparkled with gold.

We talked about what our lives had been like; we skipped over the usual small talk. I didn't have it in me. He'd had an appointment at the World Trade Center at ten o'clock on the morning of 9/11, and was on his way when the plane hit. His business partner had arrived before him and perished. He said it had taken him a long time to even start to process what it meant, to cheat death the way he had. He'd been so busy, with so many details to attend to, that in some ways he wasn't certain he'd processed it even yet.

I thought about how people handle these things differently. There are no hard and fast rules.

I said, "I know what that's like."

Eventually I told him about my aneurysm.

It turned out we had a lot in common; we both had complicated relationships with our fathers, with religion, with work.

He'd lived in a haunted house.

I'd lived in a haunted house, early in my marriage.

We rode for miles without saying anything.

He asked me if I would have dinner with him that evening. I said sure, because it felt casual and nonthreatening.

We met by the pool for a swim after biking. Another biker joined us. As we lay by the pool, all of a sudden I burst out laughing.

"I was talking to an old man today," I said.

"At the farm stand. I noticed," Henry said.

"Right. He said he drove all the way from Albuquerque once a year. 'Really? Why?' I asked him. He said, 'We're here for the burgers,' but he kind of mumbled, so I wasn't sure if I'd heard him correctly. 'Burgers?' I said. 'Pardon me? Burgers?' And I sniffed the air, I didn't smell any burgers cooking. I love cheeseburgers and I have a pretty good sense of smell. And he said, *No! Birders! Birders!* We're here for the *Birdwatching!*' Then he went on to tell me all about the fantastic variety of birds that gather here, none of which I can remember."

I laughed at my own misunderstanding. Henry looked at me, a strange expression on his face. Jan, the other biker, smiled. Perhaps they thought I was nuts. But to me it was a sign of improvement.

I felt like talking to people again. A total stranger had come up to me at the farm stand and given me an armful of apples, which seemed sweet, or slightly biblical. I imagined myself as Eve in spandex and a helmet.

That night at dinner we sat next to another table of bikers. Four women.

My face felt hot.

Henry ordered wine for us. "I just want to tell you . . . our conversations . . . while we're biking . . . they're important to me."

I didn't know what to say, so I didn't say anything.

He told me that he was between jobs. He hadn't decided what he wanted to do next. He tended to let work take over his life. It seemed to be all or nothing.

He'd told me enough so that I knew he'd done well and had recently sold his business.

I said, "I think it's wrong not to use a gift you've been given. But life has to have balance."

"I have trouble with the balance part," he said.

We'd been through some similar events. And yet I didn't know where the similarities began and ended.

He asked me questions all evening about my work, my marriage, my life. Why I worked so hard, why I'd stayed in a marriage so long, why I was alone now. I could not begin to give anything but fractional answers; the truth felt loaded, complex, and unmanageable. I'd accumulated enough trauma by then that one dinner with a stranger could not contain it all. I tried to answer his questions, but by the time dessert arrived, I felt exposed and exhausted.

I didn't sleep at all that night.

• • •

Ruthie sent me an e-mail, early the next morning. She'd gotten a tattoo. She thought I'd like it.

I knew, with utter certainty, I had never given her any reason to think I would like permanent ink on her body, regardless of its meaning or discretion.

It was going to be a long day. A lot of biking, all uphill.

Henry apologized, early on in the ride. He seemed to recognize his intrusiveness of the evening before. He rode beside me, again, all day, but he kept the conversation light, topical. He went out of his way to tell funny stories, to entertain me. We spent an enjoyable day. At some point it passed briefly through my mind that perhaps I could be capable of a vacation fling, but just as quickly I decided no. I wasn't cut out for that sort of thing. And Henry was not really my type. I didn't have a type. I knew I wasn't ready. I might never be ready. I really needed some sleep.

We met again at the pool after the forty-five-mile ride into Healdsburg. He brought me water and lemonade and seemed anxious. He talked about his kids, and his concerns for them, for how they would cope with the end of his marriage.

I got into the hot tub. An older man was there who said he was biking the area with his wife. They had a son at NYU. We talked about the school, as parents do. When I got out of the hot tub, Henry said, "That guy acted like a jerk. Monopolizing you that way."

"What are you talking about? He was nice, and I was just being polite."

He paused. "Could you be less polite next time?"

Henry. Jealous. It seemed cute. Or weird. I wasn't sure which.

After dinner we walked around the town square, looking at the books in the bookshop, discussing authors.

"Would you read Alan Greenspan's memoir?" he asked me. "You seem too liberal for that."

"Of course I would. I try to read lots of things, on diverse topics. I'm interested in the economy."

I'd read a few articles about the recent problems related to the subprime mortgage market, but they didn't affect me directly. At least, they didn't yet.

Then he walked me to my door. We stood there a long time, not speaking. Something had gradually changed, a slight shift had occurred. I didn't know when, exactly. He was more attractive to me now. The courtliness, the courteousness had grown on me. His concern for my comfort seemed genuine. We'd taken a van ride, and I'd gotten carsick. Henry was miserable that he'd suggested the van ride in the first place. Or maybe his show of jealousy made me think of him in a different light. Then again, just listening to someone talk about his children reveals him in a way few discussions can. If you listen carefully, you hear a synopsis—of values, of priorities, of regrets, of where he's spent his time and his energies in life. He'd gardened with them. He'd played sports with them. And he'd grown on me.

We stared at each other. I thought, He seems like a good guy. Then again, I knew I had bad judgment. Historical evidence supported this. And you cannot know someone in three days. So I said goodnight and let myself in to my room.

I needed some sleep, but I didn't sleep that night either. My mom had called and left a message. She'd seen wildfires in California while watching the news. Was I safe? I phoned to reassure her.

I thought a lot about Henry, his obvious interest in me. I liked him. He seemed very bright. He'd lived, but more than that, he'd assimilated his experiences into a worldview that included kindness. He appeared to be a gentleman.

The next afternoon, in Yountville, we met by the pool after our ride and had the hot tub to ourselves. The high temperature made me uncomfortable, so I sat on the side.

"You know, you're the first person I've wanted to see for a second date. Since I've been separated," Henry said. He laughed. "I've had a lot of first dates."

"I know how that is," I said.

"It's taken me a while to get comfortable alone."

I nodded.

"Twenty-five years is a long time to be married," he said. I met his eyes. "Why don't you paint your nails?" he asked, out of nowhere.

I looked down at my unmanicured hands. I knew I had nothing in common with his wife.

"I wash my hands about four hundred times a day at work. My nails are soft. A manicure only lasts twenty-four hours, so it seems silly. I do it for special occasions." I shrugged. "Did you cheat on your wife?"

He shook his head. "No."

We ate dinner with the group, then left the restaurant and went for a walk. We stopped in a pub for a drink. As soon as we sat, Henry turned my barstool to face him. He took my hand and studied me intently.

"Margaret, can you live in the moment?"

I frowned slightly, while staring at his face. I thought that was what I'd been doing these past few years—living in the moment. I thought the aneurysm had changed that about me. I used to put things off, like life, like living. Now I embraced it, as much as I knew how. Sure, it was a common idiom, and yet it summed up something crucial. Wasn't that the very issue we'd been discussing these past few days on our meandering bike rides, Henry and I? Hadn't we been discussing how hard those myriad lessons had been, to take the steps we'd taken, at our age, to learn to live in the moment? Hadn't we talked about the difference between living in the moment and recklessness? Hadn't I spent the past four-plus years struggling to learn the difference myself?

"I'm not sure I know what you're asking," I said. Then he leaned very close, taking in my scent.

Much later I realized what I should have suspected then. His question had nothing to do with living in the moment, as I understood it. It had everything to do with sex, meaning sex with no strings attached. But there could be no such thing for someone like me, after all I'd been through, at that point in time, with someone like him. His question belied a type of perfidy that was fundamentally self-serving, whereby he could walk away as if it never happened. Which is what he did, eventually, and in the cruelest way possible.

Somewhere along one of those roads in the golden autumn of Napa Valley, I'd made an assumption that Henry's brush with death had been similar to my brush with death, but it turns out these things can affect people differently.

For some people a brush with death means a prod to have that plastic surgery they've been putting off. For some, it's a reassurance that their life choices were correct to that point—like divine recognition of their personal merit. For others, it turns out to be a gift that keeps on giving, a gradual, sometimes tortured, revelation. But some skip over lessons learned altogether and take what they can from it, in the worst possible sense. Neither medicine nor motherhood had prepared me to anticipate the casual deceits that came easily to the lips of a man who used his near-death experience to seduce me; I did not possess that radar. Perhaps such deceit flourishes on Wall Street—in business, in investment banking, or in the legal profession; in my field of medicine, deceit is deadly. And in motherhood—well, I didn't teach my kids to lie.

The only thing I can compare it to is dog hearing; I should listen at a different frequency level, not just to what men say but for the assurances they imply, for all they omit, for the questions they expertly skirt, and for the information they seem to be getting at when they're trying to get at me.

So I need some sort of hearing device—a hearing-ear dog, perhaps. Do they have those? Could I possibly train my sweet Olga? I know she'd protect me if she could.

But I did not have one then, not when I needed it most.

"I really care about you, Margaret," Henry said. "How do you feel about me?"

"I like you too." Then he kissed me.

Chapter Twenty

THE LIGHTS ALONG the running path still flash when I walk past. I've learned to take this binary system of communication with the dead for the gift that it is, and say thank you. Thank you very much. Sometimes I channel Elvis. One night not long ago, in the cool smart autumn air with leaves crunching underfoot, Olga and I walked down to our favorite light and I thought about Paul, my late anesthesiologist friend. His heart attack had been on Memorial Day, but he died suddenly on New Year's Eve 1996.

My partner Martin had called with the news.

Stig, Bea, Ruthann, and I had rented in a condo in Deer Valley, Utah, for the holiday week. Skiing obsessed me back then, though I was a novice. I wanted the kids to learn while they were young, so that they would feel natural on skis. I took them whenever I could. I loved the cold, the quiet, the balance and peace, the health of it. But this trip felt doomed from the beginning.

It seemed like there were doctors everywhere—in the lift lines discussing antihypertensive medications, in the midmountain cafeteria lines discussing neurosurgical techniques, in the après-ski lounge bar flirting with the hookers while pretending to be insurance salesmen from Des Moines. Bad enough that I lived with a doctor and worked with many, but even at 8,500 feet I could not escape them. I'd never traveled so far to run into so many obnoxious people I knew.

The condo we rented had no hot water due to a malfunctioning pilot light on the water heater.

Huge crowds aggravated already poor mountain conditions, so the snow grew soft and slushy. On the second day of skiing, I emerged from a chairlift with my tips crossed and ended up sprawled inelegantly on my butt with legs spread-eagled and skis crossing at a 120-degree angle. I pulled the medial collateral ligament in my left knee, which, though painful, was not a serious handicap from a mechanical standpoint. It only hurt when I skied.

On New Year's Eve we ate an early dinner in a faux Bavarian restaurant where the entertainment consisted of a grown man in lederhosen playing an eight-foot horn.

Shortly after midnight the phone woke me. In our household, the phone routinely rang 24/7 due to the nature of our work. But that night I sat up in bed, alert, absolutely certain that something terrible had happened. Sometimes you just know.

Martin had tracked me down through my parents.

"Margaret." Martin spoke in clipped tones. "I'm sorry to call you so late, but I've got bad news. Paul died tonight. He had a cardiac arrhythmia."

I placed a shaky hand over my own thumping heart.

"What is it?" Stig reached out, arm bumping my knee in the dark.

"Paul's dead," I whispered.

"He was out with Julie," Martin said, referring to Paul's date that night, a nurse we worked with. "They went to a movie and then back to her place. They were sitting in her living room, and he told her he didn't feel well, then rolled his eyes back and slumped over. She did CPR, and the paramedics arrived within three minutes, but they couldn't save him. Julie called from the ER, and I went over. He looked pretty peaceful."

"He looked peaceful?" I repeated. I felt stupid, and numb.

"Yeah. They had trouble getting the tube in, believe it or not. I never thought of Paul as a difficult intubation, did you?" He meant the endotracheal tube, the breathing tube, the one that goes into the windpipe, breathes for you, sustains your oxygen. Putting that tube in is part of our specialty—it's what we do.

"Uh, no," I answered, picturing Paul's airway from the side. His jaw length, his mandibular anatomy.

How could he be dead?

I hung up and leaned back against the headboard. My hands were damp, my mouth dry. Heavy drapes blocked out the snowy light of nighttime in the Wasatch Mountains; the room was nearly black. I stared ahead into the crushing darkness. How could he look anything but peaceful? Dead is dead, isn't it? I couldn't grasp the loss of him. It wasn't possible. It wasn't right.

What would I do?

"I'm really sorry, honey," Stig said. "I always wondered why they didn't put a defibrillator in him when he had that heart attack in May. There's early anecdotal evidence that says young people with big heart attacks and low ejection fractions should be treated empirically with implantable defibrillators, even without doing electro-physiologic studies."

Stig always talked like that. He had a lot of calm, clinical, business-as-usual experience with death.

I didn't say anything.

In his own way, he meant to say Paul didn't have to die. From a cardiac standpoint, anyway. Technically. I should take comfort.

After a while I heard Stig snoring again. I lay awake, stunned and lonelier than ever. Then in a corner of the room, near the ceiling, a strange but intense bright light flickered. I sat up and looked around for the source, some small metal fragment, a watch perhaps, but there was nothing to cause it. The light moved then, deliberately, oddly, and I slowly came to realize it was Paul—or his spirit, anyway. He was there in the room with me, while Stig slept, letting me say good-bye, saying good-bye to me. Perhaps he had more to say, but I didn't know it then. The light danced, flickering about, moving from ceiling to floor and back, to the left, then the right across the ceiling, like a slightly sedated or slightly demented Tinker Bell.

His death had been too sudden. It's not good to die unprepared. Was he prepared? I worried about his spirit, I suppose, but mostly I worried about me. I'd lost him, I'd lost my friend; he was my tether, one of my few connections to sanity in the terrifying environment of a major urban trauma center, in the terrifying environment of life. I'd lost my God-brother.

I watched the light skitter around the room until I drifted off to sleep. When I woke some hours later, it was gone.

Chapter Twenty-one

I'm on trauma call, it's after midnight, and I'm going to lie down to rest, but the anesthesia library smells like onions from a leftover lunch brought by a drug rep, and the way I spent my day today is too haunting to let me sleep. Sometimes I feel a little like a voyeur in this job, like someone who watches life from the periphery, an observer to the pain and suffering, not really able to help, just a bystander with a pocketful of medications.

When Paul was alive, every morning he'd say to me, "Be careful out there." He knew the perfect advice to give a fellow anesthesiologist; our profession depends on diligence and attention. As in life, so much of the rest is luck. Some days it feels as though we walk through a battlefield, dodging bullets.

Every patient I've taken care of today has been lost, in one way or another. First an AIDS patient with anal condyloma or warts needed them lasered off. We wore special masks to prevent us from breathing in the virus as it was vaporized.

The next patient was an alcoholic whose knee had been torn up in an accident but came into the hospital prior to his surgery to undergo detox to make the procedure safe. I interviewed the patient in presurgery. He answered all my questions, understood the nature of the anesthetic. He told me he drank a fifth of vodka a day. His wife sat in a chair beside the hospital cart. They were both young, from Eastern Europe.

"Aren't you going to give him something to help his nerves?" she asked, her voice strident, tinged with anger.

We've gotten away from premedicating patients, unless the nurses think it necessary. When they admit the patients to presurgery, they get a good feel for their anxiety level, then let us know. Our nurses are experienced, and we depend on their judgment. Often the interview itself calms patients. When someone slips by who seems to need a sedative, the nurses are happy to provide one on our orders.

This alcoholic knee patient was calm, and we don't premedicate family members. The wife defined codependency.

Every patient is not just a patient but a family. Though the anal condyloma patient came alone, he too represented a family, conspicuous in its absence.

While I was going through my divorce, I paid particular attention to the couples who came to the hospital and the surgical center. I watched how they supported each other, and often asked how long they'd been together. I liked to get them talking about their marriages, and their lives together, how they'd met, how they spent their time, how many kids they had, and grandkids. I tried to learn something, though I wasn't too sure what it was I learned. I saw devotion between partners, sometimes regardless of years spent together. It gave me hope when I needed it.

My last patient today—a would-be suicide from two months ago—was a seventy-one-year-old who tried to kill himself with a gunshot to the head and had succeeded only in blowing off his face, completely missing his brain. He left a note saying that he had been given a diagnosis of Alzheimer's disease. The paramedics had told us that his wife had recently died. He'd been told he would lose his home. He said he did not want to live institutionalized. Could you blame him? Today he had a sixteen-hour procedure to try to rebuild a jawbone. He has no nose.

We've had a run of these lately—suicide patients who would have died except for expert emergency medical services in the field. The recent spate of patients admitted as suicides were not people who'd exhibited suicidal gestures—they were the real things gone awry. My last call, a couple weeks ago, I had a slightly younger man who took a box cutter to his own throat, after failing at his wrists. We get these patients all the time. People jumping off buildings and bridges, onto highways, drinking Drano, stabbing themselves in the abdomen or the neck, trying to scalp themselves. The violence, the depression, the profound depression that exists out there astonishes.

But why should it? Life is damaging. Personally, I have support systems and a therapist and an education and a meaningful job and my health. I know to exercise when my anxiety level mounts. I have friends to call, sisters who will meet me for dinner and spend the night at my house if I really need help. I try to imagine what it must be like for those without access to therapy, and medical care, and medication, and just the simple open-mindedness that recognizes depression as an illness instead of a deliberate state of mind, or laziness. Ignorance for the afflicted is a death sentence. Our scalped patient had just been released from prison. Prison! Talk about hopelessness. One man, no education, a prison record, a bad economy— what are his options? Who will give him a chance?

In medical school, I had an oncology patient, a schoolteacher I grew close to, dying of breast cancer. Her oncologist taught me an important lesson as I helplessly watched my patient struggle to breathe: "Don't just do something, stand there," he told me. I will never forget those words and it's not really apropos of anything anymore—I don't get paid to stand there—but the lesson is metaphorical anyway. I have learned to offer the comforting solidity of my own presence*; sometimes that means comforting the patient, sometimes comforting the surgeon during the sixteen-hour operation on the man who shot off his own face because the surgeon doesn't even know why he's bothering to operate on someone who doesn't want to live; sometimes it's the staff who only know how to make dark jokes. I guess the point is that somewhere along the way, I learned about my own value as a physician if nothing else, and as a person, as someone who is willing to hold the hand of another in need, recognizing that the one in need may or may not always be the patient. I don't know if the divorce or the aneurysm or the lights in the park or maybe in some strange dark way even the rape did that for me. My career saved me time and again.

As a younger person, a younger physician, I struggled against the limits of compassion, my own and others'. I thought, compassion is not enough. I didn't have the words, I didn't have the ability to speak real words of comfort. Words limited me. Now I know that words don't matter. Showing up is enough. Like Cal Ripken, showing up is everything.

Paul came to dinner three months before he died, after his bypass surgery. I found a recipe for low-fat enchiladas and made two types

---

*Adapted from Acharya Eric Spiegel.

of guacamole. One guacamole had lots of vegetables, the other one had regular old avocado. He ignored the low-fat and slathered the better-tasting guacamole on his enchiladas and took seconds.

We talked about medicine. This was autumn 1996.

"Some days," I said, "I don't know what I'm doing. I don't know who I'm helping. I wonder if I made the right choice."

"What are you talking about?" he asked.

"I know what she means," Stig said. "I feel like anybody could do this job."

"You guys are assholes," Paul said, leaning forward. He put his elbows on the table. I sent the kids upstairs to do their homework. "Every day I help people. Every day I make someone better, some-how, some way. If you don't believe that, you have no business doing what you're doing."

I felt chastened. I don't know what Stig felt. But afterward, years later, I recognized the difference between Paul and myself at that point. Paul had been a patient. When Paul lay in the ICU, he'd been on the receiving end of medical care. And he wasn't there for something slight, or simple, for a knee scope or a carpal tunnel. He was there for a life-threatening illness, like a brain aneurysm. It had changed something fundamental about him, and ultimately it changed how he felt about patients, how he treated and related to patients.

The same was true about me now.

Chapter Twenty-two

THE LAST DAY of my Napa bike trip, on the way to breakfast, I ran into Mitchell. Yes, Mitchell, the attorney, the man I had dated less than a year earlier for six weeks, who had walked out of my condo claiming our relationship was "too perfect," the man who was the final straw before I changed my life forever. We were almost two thousand miles from home. He walked toward me with a blonde-haired woman on his arm. She looked a little like me.

"Margaret?"

"Mitchell!"

"What are you doing in Yountville?"

Since I was outfitted in biking gear, head to toe, this seemed a fairly stupid question, but I smiled. What else could I do? This is my life.

"I'm on a bike trip through Napa Valley. Today is our last day, then we're off to San Francisco. What are you doing here?"

"We're here for a business meeting." The woman on his arm cleared her throat.

Mitchell glanced at her, I glanced at her, then he said, "Margaret, I want to introduce you to my friend."

An awkward silence ensued. He said, "Uh, I mean, uh, my fiancée, Karen."

With the smile affixed to my face, I did not miss a beat. I held out my hand and shook hers, as befitted the soul of graciousness that I'd become. Karen looked like she had sucked a lemon. "It's so nice to meet you. Congratulations to you both."

I continued to smile while Mitchell said something or other, but my thoughts went elsewhere, mostly upstairs to the meta-chamber, where they tended to go in these situations. I wondered, What is this all about? What are the odds? God, Paul, somebody, are you trying to tell me something?

I said good-bye, and actually walked away from Mitchell and Karen, toward breakfast, raised my eyes and my arms to heaven, and said, out loud, "What?!? What was that all about? What are you trying to tell me? There are no running path lights out here, so I need some help!"

And of course, much later, in retrospect, I realized what God or Paul was trying to tell me. He was trying to tell me, too succinctly in point of fact, that my new friend Henry would do the same thing to me that Mitchell had done. He would walk out the door one day without a backward glance, for some contrived reason, and I would never hear from him again. But I was not smart enough to heed the very obvious, very direct divine intervention. Because I was younger then and still stupid. This was, after all, a few years ago.

Later that day, when I told Henry about running into Mitchell, about the way Mitchell had ended things, Henry asked me, "Why would you want to be with a man who was capable of treating you like that?"

Why indeed?

Henry's divorce commenced soon after the Napa Valley trip. We saw each other three times over the next four months, and we spoke nearly every day on the phone. He came to Chicago twice; we met in Florida once. I never went to New York. A couple of times plans fell through because of the weather or our kids. He spent some time with my mom, who liked him. He met my kids, who reserved judgment due to my abysmal track record. I agreed with them in theory—I felt I wasn't rushing into something. How could I? We lived in different states, and Henry had a long road in front of him. So I stayed cautious and circumspect, or I thought I did. The lights in the park remained lit when we walked Olga at night, and I saw bunnies everywhere. The significance of the rabbits eluded me; at least they weren't rats. Things felt right when we were together, though I knew better than to think that meant anything. Something crept up on me, though, and I understood the saying—*my other half*—for the only time in my life. But like I said, I remained cautious, I knew it didn't mean much. It was too soon for that.

One night in late January, we went to see the movie *The Diving Bell and the Butterfly*, the story of Jean-Dominique Bauby, a former editor-in-chief of *Elle* magazine who suffered a massive stroke and developed "locked-in syndrome," a horrible condition of near total paralysis in which he had movement of only his eyes, one of which was sewn shut. The stroke left his thought processes intact. I'd read the book and seen a patient with this syndrome early in my career, so the movie affected me. It seemed to affect Henry too. After having dinner with Hayley and Daniel, we took Olga for a walk.

"What did you think of the scene where Bauby snubs the mother of his children in favor of his young girlfriend, even though the girlfriend had never been to visit him at the hospital?" Henry asked me. "Didn't that bother you? After all he'd been through, he was still a jerk."

I thought about Henry's questions. The scene had stayed with me too, but not for the same reason. "Just because someone has a catastrophic experience doesn't mean it changes who he is," I answered, thinking out loud. "It doesn't change his basic personality. What Schnabel [the director] seemed to be getting at was that being near death made Bauby want to redeem himself. I think the movie is about the redemptive power of art. Here this guy goes through a horrendous experience, can only blink one eye, and manages to write a book about what it's like to live that way. The experience doesn't change the facts of his personality, doesn't turn him into a saint, but it provides him with the impetus to create something permanent to leave behind after he's gone. He still wants to be the guy he was before the stroke, with the sports car and the twenty-year-old girlfriend. But the guy who has suffered the stroke uses what he knows best, which is to write, as a final act of redemption."

Later, after Henry suddenly and without warning told me he couldn't see me again, I struggled to understand how a man who seemed to have depth, who seemed to care so much, could turn into someone who could simply switch off his heart. I would remember that night, that conversation, and wonder if the answer wasn't there in his words, if only I could decode what he was really saying to me. Did Henry project his own issues onto Bauby, his guilt about leaving his wife, his lack of resolution over his own brush with death? Did he simply want to date younger women? We were in the middle of planning another trip. We'd both bought plane tickets. Then, one day, in the middle of discussing hotel reservations, he said he couldn't see me anymore. He said his lawyer recommended it. I suspect that's another way of saying it was all about money. But Henry never explained. His coldness stunned me. I sent him an invitation to my fiftieth birthday party six weeks later but he declined. He sent a note wishing me a happy birthday and telling me he hoped I'd have a nice decade. I never heard from him again.

Who was Henry from New York?

Perhaps he was just a guy traumatized by the prospect of a messy divorce, by the pain of the unknown, scared shitless like the rest of us. He had only begun a process that I was completing; he faced a long journey up a dangerous river that would exact a high price and that doubtless would be apocalyptic. The jungle awaited him, where he would likely do more than his share of collateral damage. Perhaps he took the easier path, turned back, and never made the journey at all. Perhaps I ignored my own maxim: good manners do not signify a good person. Or perhaps my own trauma prevented me from seeing that he was never the man I'd thought he was.

In the end, it was my misfortune to meet Henry in the wrong place at the wrong time and to not recognize his singular code of ethics, or his extraordinary acting skills. I would have given him a wide berth. Certain people sneak past your guard.

I feel quite confident that you the reader would like a Hollywood ending to this story. As the writer, I wish I could give it to you. But I'm afraid you would need to think in terms of independent films, documentaries, or experimental films, and not your typical big-studio romance. Life never turns out the way we plan it.

• • •

My fiftieth birthday came and went. I partied, but in the big scheme of things it was just another day.

Kate remarried. Her husband is also widowed and they seem happy. We all miss Neal, and I think of him every time I get on my bike or bake something wonderful from a recipe out of *Bon Appetit*.

My mother's dementia has progressed rapidly over the past two years, and she requires full-time care now. It has been a heart-breaking process to watch, though worse for her, as she has had a sense of her ongoing loss. Several times she said to me, "It's a terrible thing to lose your mind, Margaret." As her dementia progressed, her anxiety progressed. When she finally reached a point of profound memory loss, she became happier. She's finally calm after a lifetime of worry. I visit her once or twice a week, tell her stories, and try to make her laugh. She has not yet lost her sense of humor, but I miss her, the fundamental person of her. That part has slowly slipped away.

My daughters, four years post divorce, eight years post separation, now thrive. Bea worked a few years after college, but gradually found her focus. She moved home and has gone back to school to become a doctor. Of all things.

Ruthie graduated from college last spring. She graduated on the dean's list, with a degree in liberal arts, though I could not say what she majored in. Maybe because of her accident, or in spite of it, I think she has a head start on life.

Their paths look remarkably different from mine, and I'm grateful for that.

• • •

Olga turned thirteen in the fall and remains as gentle and loving as ever. We still share peanut butter and jelly sandwiches for dinner on occasion, then take slow walks together each night, checking out the park with its bunnies and squirrels, raccoons and rats, checking out the lights. She has trouble making it all the way down to the running path most nights, as her hips are sore with arthritis. But on occasion, when she's feeling frisky, we meander down to our favorite spot and are rewarded with a blink.

In my quest to understand this journey, I changed therapists, ironically opting for a man. I needed a positive relationship with just one intelligent and empathic male, a kind of *surrogate guy*, in the hope that he might help me really comprehend how men think, to prevent endless bitterness, and to access my anger. I wanted to avoid emerging from the jungle permanently scarred, dismembered, or simply beheaded. I needed to understand the how and the why, get past the who, and decipher the what-the-fuck.

I definitely have scars, but my head appears to be intact. I keep a picture of Saint Denis on my computer to remind myself of what might have been.

I stopped "dating" after Henry. I began writing in earnest, and in doing so, I recognized my own patterns of behavior, behavior that seems obvious and destructive in retrospect. I gave up the Internet, though friends still tell me it's the only way for a woman my age to meet a man. I find that incredibly depressing. Occasionally I convince myself they're right; I sign up, pay for three months, quit after a day or two. The trauma of my marriage and divorce made me believe, at some level, either conscious or not, that love was dangerous, and so I found men who were unavailable, unappealing, or just plain wrong for me. But now that I recognize the tendency, I've begun to allow myself friendships instead, and consequently I feel more positive than I have in years about life and about men. Even so, I think that it takes at least six months to know someone well enough to begin to let hope triumph over experience, to take the tiniest leap of faith, or to go without the assistance of my "hearing-ear" dog.

And from friendship, love can grow. I feel certain that will be the right kind of love, the kind that grows from the inside out. Only time will tell. Only time allows trust to develop.

Growing old is not for sissies.

It took fifty years of living and writing things down and way too much therapy before I learned that some people will do anything to get what they want, and I need to avoid them. But if you, like me, can survive your own middle-age trauma, you might move on to a chapter of life that you think of as wisdom, since it sounds more appealing than dotage. On bad days I think I've made every mistake out there and know to anticipate the worst. On good days I know how lucky I am to be alive. Every day I wish that wisdom were not accompanied by receding gums, memory loss, and joint deterioration.

At some point I began writing letters to Paul, telling him stories about everything that had happened to me from the day I left Stig. Since Paul seemed to be communicating with me through the lights in the park at night, I decided I would speak to him in a more coherent fashion. Somehow those letters turned into this.

As to my own trip on the river, chugging along, breathing the fumes, and dodging bullets, life feels as tenuous as ever. Humans are tough, for the most part. It's life that's fragile.

Everything can change in a heartbeat; it can slip away from you in an instant. Everything you trust, and treasure, whatever brings you comfort, comes at a terrible cost. Health is temporary; money disappears. Safety is nothing but an illusion.

So when the moment comes, and everything you depend upon changes, or perhaps someone you love disappears, or no longer loves you, must disaster follow? Or will you—somehow—adapt?

These are big questions, I think, but answerable. If you reduce them to their simplest forms, if you reduce many existential questions to their simplest forms, and you ask the questions in just the right way, then put them to someone who might know, you get a yes or no answer. For example: *Does disaster always follow?* Or *Can I adapt?* Put as a binary question, the answer requires no algebra, no trigonometry, no quadratic equations. It could not be simpler. Which means, I guess, if you were to wait until dark to walk in the park tonight, you'd have an important and meaningful question to ask of the lights. Just have patience. It can take time, and practice, and a little bit of faith to decipher their response.

Acknowledgments

Many, many thanks go to my wonderful daughters for reading and believing, and to Karen, Cindy, Mary, Larry, Lydia, Kathy, David, Claudia, Rick, Doti, Mary Kay, Jere, Jeff, Karen and Nick, Laurie, Mom, Carp, Vicki, Cliff, George, Joe I., Joe L., Marylou, the wonderful staff at GSC, and the rest of my family, friends, and coworkers (you know who you are!) for living through the experiences that became this book.

I am deeply indebted to Pat Toomay in particular for reading from the very beginning, generously, and for believing. Other patient and generous readers to whom I owe a big TY include Allison Burnett, Karen Schneider, Jocelyn, Gary Kroeger, Beth Kohl, and Bill Miller. Special thanks go to Janet Desaulniers, James McManus, Barbara, and Mark for inspiration and for believing that I had a story to tell.

Lisa Bankoff, you are simply awesome, the best ever.

Thank you, Nancy Miller, for your unstinting encouragement, for teasing out the best possible version of this story, and for making me think it through just one more time. Special thanks go to everyone at Bloomsbury for their support.

And finally, I owe a huge debt of gratitude to Patrick Fanning for finding a way to get me days off when I needed to write.

—*Margaret Overton*

A NOTE ON THE AUTHOR

MARGARET OVERTON is an anaesthetist with an MFA in writing from the School of the Art Institute of Chicago. Her work has appeared in the *Chicago Tribune Sunday Magazine* and *Creative Nonfiction*. She lives in Chicago, and *Good in a Crisis* is her first book.

In Memory of
Lydia Overton
1917–2010